Representations of Poverty in Videogames

"*Representations of Poverty in Videogames* is a must-read book for any scholar interested in the intersection of video games, poverty studies, and player experience. Crowley provides a compellingly precise argument that clarifies the often-murky concept of poverty as deployed in the study of video games. His insights will prompt all of us to rethink concepts like poverty, lore, slumming, romance, and economy in the games we play and study."

—Mike Piero, *Professor of English, Cuyahoga Community College, USA*, and author of *Video Game Chronotopes and Social Justice: Playing on the Threshold* (Palgrave, 2021)

Adam Crowley

Representations of Poverty in Videogames

palgrave
macmillan

Adam Crowley
Husson University
Bangor, ME, USA

ISBN 978-3-031-00146-8 ISBN 978-3-031-00144-4 (eBook)
https://doi.org/10.1007/978-3-031-00144-4

Cover illustration: Jon Helgason / Alamy Stock Photo

This Palgrave Macmillan imprint is published by the registered company Springer Nature Switzerland AG.
The registered company address is: Gewerbestrasse 11, 6330 Cham, Switzerland

This book is dedicated to my wife, Sojourner, and my daughter, Una.

Acknowledgments

This book would not have been possible without the support and guidance of Shaun Vigil, Camille Davies, Imogen Higgins, and the other members of Palgrave Macmillan I had the pleasure of interacting with during the drafting process. Additionally, Husson University played a significant role and provided me with the time and space that was necessary for this work to occur: Patricia Bixel, Philp Taylor, Greg Winston, David Haus, and others were all supportive in various capacities and at various times. Similarly, the University of Maine helped to facilitate this work—students, staff, and colleagues in the UM Honors College were a constant source of encouragement for me. Additionally, the Popular Culture Association and several of its regional affiliates provided an exciting and charged atmosphere for the individual arguments that, over time, became the book you are holding. My family has been my greatest source of support.

Contents

CHAPTER 1

Introduction

Game Studies and Poverty

To the extent that videogames share common characteristics that extend beyond individual acts of play, they might be associated with general notions of form. Questions concerned with such notions were, as noted by Jesper Juul, particularly relevant to then-nascent field of game studies at the turn of the century. Juul describes the period as "something of a gold rush and a race toward being the first to point out special aspects of games, to format the field and define words, and to point to similarities and dissimilarities between games and other cultural forms."[1] Without being unnecessarily dismissive of the field's developmental period, it is the case that, today, scholars still publishing in the disciple might characterize Juul's supposed "gold rush" with another, quite distinct West Coast reference—the Donner Party. Failing to attend to the boundaries of their own analytical schemes, droves of scholars headed into the emerging field quite certain of their prospects—and vanished, at least with respect to the citation records associated with any number of discipline-specific publications that emerged after the Great Recession (2007–2009).

During the second and now third decade of our century, productive efforts to historicize videogames, such as those that are offered by Carly A. Kocurek (2015) and Michael Z. Newman (2017), have—at least for the moment—deflated the notion that the videogame form is a precise subject that aches for novel definition. Rather, and in growing numbers,

A. Crowley, *Representations of Poverty in Videogames*,
https://doi.org/10.1007/978-3-031-00144-4_1

scholars instead contend with questions of development and purpose: that is to say, what are the industrial, technological, and social conditions of the player's act of play, and how might these conditions find expression in what Ian Bogost has identified as the "procedural rhetoric" of digital entertainment?[2] From time to time, works associated with this notion imply that videogames have become a meaningful vehicle for representing contemporary, middle-class anxieties about poverty in the United States: for example, Nick Dyer-Witheford and Greig de Peuter's *Games of Empire* (2009) and Randy Nichols' *The Video Game Business* (2014) provide meaningful contexts for such assumptions. These and related works have emerged alongside a number of arguments that address—sometimes broadly and sometimes with remarkable clarity—the subject of play aesthetics: for example, Tamer Thabet's *Video Game Narrative and Criticism: Playing the Story* (2015), Souvik Mukherjee's *Video Games and Storytelling: Reading Games and Playing Books* (2015), Timothy J. Welsh's *Mixed Realism: Videogames and the Violence of Fiction* (2017), and Darshana Jayemanne's *Performativity in Art, Literature, and Videogames* (2017). In the following chapter, and indeed throughout this book, the primary goal is to explore and synthesize key conceptions of players and poverty in such works, for the purpose of specifying discipline-specific understandings of these subjects.

Throughout, the major arguments are framed by—and often dependent upon—an established and expanding area of inquiry concerned with identity in gaming cultures, and they aim to address a need for criticism that applies such considerations to aesthetic traditions that pre-date and continue to inform the act of play in digital environments. This need originates in early reflections on the videogame form from scholars including Janet H. Murray (1997), Alexander Galloway (2004), Edward Castronova (2005), McKenzie Wark (2009), Ian Bogost (2010), and others who regard the interactive nature of videogames as one of the form's definitive features. In the recent past, a number of scholars have expanded upon these and similar notions with thoughtful considerations of the form's relevance to various demographics within the United States: for example, Adrienne Shaw (2015), Shira Chess (2017), and Megan Condis (2018). In such efforts, there is a notable, shared conversation about class and its relevance to gaming cultures, one that resonates with select publications listed above that are explicitly concerned with the relevance of capitalism to the player's act of play. Significant onto themselves, these efforts have additional and to-date unexplored implications for a number of essays that address notions of class consciousness in popular videogames from a range of major publishers including Blizzard Entertainment (Snodgrass 2016; Pearce 2017); *Rockstar Games* (Stark 2010); *BioWare* (Geraci 2014; Krobová et al. 2015; Hayden 2017); and *Bethesda* (Moberly & Moberly). Taken together, these works and their intersecting concerns suggest a meaningful trajectory for game studies scholarship in the early to mid-2020s.

Poverty in *Woke* Game Studies Discourse

The topic of poverty and its relevance to videogames is a developing—but presently underdeveloped—subject of academic inquiry. For scholars concerned with such matters, Kishonna Gray and David J. Leonard's *Woke Gaming: Digital Challenges to Oppression and Social Injustice* (2018) is perhaps the most relevant work—as of this writing. In that collection, "poverty" is a named concept relevant to three essays. In each instance, the term is deployed in ways that speak to its emerging but limited relevance to game studies. The first instance occurs deep into Timothy Rowlands et al.'s "Power, Violence, and the Mask: Representations of Criminal Subjectivity in *Grand Theft Auto Online*." There, the authors include poverty by way of a block quote from J.P. Gee's *Good Video Games + Good Learning: Collected Essays on Video Games, Learning and Literacy* (2007). Gee yokes poverty with the concept of crime for the purpose of noting the relevance of both to *Grand Theft Auto: San Andreas.*[3] From this position, Gee goes on to observe that while the concepts are relevant to the title, the game is much more interested in directing the player to engage in petty bourgeois activities like bike riding and map navigation than it is in addressing the visible effects of poverty and crime on San Andreas. Subsequently, he uses the term as an opportunity to describe an alternative version of the game, one in which the player takes photos of people instead of shooting them or delivers messages instead of explosives. In total, the comments are more particular to the issue of crime than poverty: Gee is concerned with how to reduce or remove illegal activities from the game. Rowlands et al. take Gee's comments as being instructive for their own efforts to rationalize "alternative content" opportunities for gameplay.[4]

The second and related use of poverty in the collection emerges in Karen Skardzius' "Playing with Pride: Claiming Space Through Community Building in *World of Warcraft.*" Well into her argument,

Skardzius deploys a quote from Judith Butler as part of a larger effort to extend and complicate Butler's theory of precarity. Skardzius quotes Butler as asserting that precarious populations are "at heightened risk of disease, poverty, starvation, displacement, and of exposure to violence without protection."[5] Skardzius then draws from Jensen and De Castell to note that "playing, creating, or consuming video games obviously does not come with the risk of death due to starvation or poor living conditions that Butler speaks to in her work," but then goes on to add that such issues, to the extent they extend to violence and aggression, are a "very real problem" for women in the videogame industry and LGBTQ players in *World of Warcraft*.[6] As was the case for Rowlands et al., poverty here emerges in relation to another or associated subject: crime for Roland et al. and the above listing of calamites for Skardzius.

The third use of the term in the collection appears in Taylor Anderson-Barkley and Kira Foglesong's "Activism in Video Games: A New Voice for Social Change." As was the case in the above examples, the term first emerges well into the argument—and in the context of a quote—in this case from David J. Leonard in "Not a Hater, Just Keepin' It Real: The Importance of Race- and Gender-Based Game Studies" (2006). In that piece, Leonard argues that stereotypical portrayals in videogames can "make racism, sexism, and poverty appear to be natural, normal, and inevitable part [sic] of everyday life."[7] The authors use the quote as an opportunity to defend the discursive capacities of videogames, which the authors value as significant if titles are capable of conveying and affirming such notions. Here, too, the concept emerges in association with one or more related concepts—racism and sexism.

The rhetorical similarities these essays share with respect to the concept of poverty and its deployment point toward a common but probably unintentional function for the term in *Woke Gaming*. Generally, that function can be described as a concept addressed through citations that conceptualize poverty in association with one or more related social ills. Those ills are highlighted for the purpose of justifying an observation or concern that affirms the exigence of the argument at hand, and these affirmations are typically quite general and left unspecified and undefended. This patterning is certainly not a shortcoming in any of these essays, as none of the authors assert that poverty is itself a central concept in their respective arguments. Indeed, and quite to the contrary, the use of quoted material to introduce the concept in each argument is productive to the extent that it suggests novel ground for future clarifications of earlier scholarship founded in or relevant to game studies.

To further underscore the point, it should be noted that the concept of poverty itself is no more relevant to the works these essays cite than it is to the actual essays included in *Woke Gaming*. Gee's *Good Video Games + Good Learning: Collected Essays on Video Games, Learning and Literacy* only raises the term one other time and in the context of a general aside.[8] Butler does not raise the concept again in "Performativity, Precarity and Sexual Politics." The same can be said of David J. Leonard in "Not a Hater, Just Keepin' It Real: The Importance of Race- and Gender-Based Game Studies" (2006). In this broader context, the concept of poverty appears to have entered into game studies discourse almost by accident—the term is scooped up with other, related concepts to help these authors mark an incremental advancement in their larger arguments.

It is equally important to note that none of these works deploy the term as a specified concept—that is to say, poverty is presented with assumed but tacit values. The nature of those values can be inferred from the concepts that are tied to the term in its various appearances: for example, crime, sexism, and racism. This use of the term is consistent with respect to the list of references each author above associates with his or her scholarship. Given the relatively minor role the concept of poverty plays in Gray and Leonard's edited collection, it is reasonable to ask whether or not the field is calling for specific conceptions of the term. After all, in each of the three relevant essays, poverty might reasonably be extracted from the identified sentences without changing the nature or purpose of each sentence's role, in terms of how it supports one or more points in its respective essay.

Critical Contexts of Poverty in Game Studies Scholarship

However, a broader consideration of the field—especially older scholarship—suggests that contemporary game studies scholarship like the kind offered in *Woke Gaming* would benefit from specified understandings of poverty. This inference can be made by considering a collection of texts with long-standing relevance to the field: Janet H. Murray's *Hamlet on the Holodeck: The Future of Narrative in Cyberspace* (1997), Edward Castronova's *Synthetic Worlds: The Business and Culture of Online Games*

(2005), and Nick Dyer-Witheford and Grieg de Peuter's *Games of Empire: Global Capitalism and Video Games* (2009). The concept of poverty does not emerge in Murray's work, but Murray sets the stage for later conversation with her early, non-specific comments on the economics of digital storytelling. She notes that "the technical and economic cultivation of this fertile new medium of communication has led to several new varieties of narrative entertainment"[9] and later returns to this observation with something of a warning for videogame players. Writing of the possible futures for the videogame industry in the late 1990s, she writes, "Although economic and social forces may never move the established game industry far past the lucrative shoot-'em-ups and puzzle mazes, there is no reason why more sophisticated developers could not make stories that have more dramatic human resonance and human import to them."[10] It is an interesting and telling assertion, one that does not name poverty but summons it to mind, to the extent it suggests that, generally, those to whom the videogame industry caters will have access to titles that lack the "human import" of titles developed by "more sophisticated developers," presumably for more specialized audiences. Elsewhere, she begins to tease out another important possibility when she notes that future gameplay may involve players acting out or affirming certain economic anxieties in the course of play: considering a hypothetical *Casablanca* simulation, she writes of characters with "overlapping states of mind (e.g., related to inebriation, infatuation, desire of economic security, and awareness of physical vulnerability)."[11] However, and as is reasonable given how non-specific Murray's use of economics is in her text, she concludes her argument with the assertion that "we cannot yet predict the economics of the television-internet merger."[12] While she remains non-specific, Murray raises the specter of economics to suggest two noteworthy possibilities: that consumption will be tied to industry practices bearing on financial possibilities and that gameplay might be conceptualized in ways that take into account the economic concerns of the player in his or her acts of play. While these notions are rather unremarkable in the context of Murray's larger argument, they set the stage of interpretive possibilities that have had a noteworthy impact on game studies, an impact that year after year has been developing to a point that would justify specified conversations around the topic of poverty.

For example, the concept of poverty only emerges one time in Edward Castronova's *Synthetic Worlds: The Business and Culture of Online Games* (2005). It emerges as part of an earnest but rather lame joke. Castronova imagines a game titled *El Dorado*,[13] in which resources are plentiful. The game draws players away from other imagined games, games in which resources are less plentiful: i.e., "*World of Poverty, World of Want.*"[14] While Castronova does not attend to the concept directly, he approaches the subject of poverty through his detailed consideration of "fun economies" in games.[15] According to Castronova, fun economies "give people a meaningful role to play"[16] in a game and "allows you to feel like you own a little piece of the world."[17] He then argues, much as Murray suggests when she considers "overlapping states of mind" in the *Casablanca* simulation, that fun economies should have "property, theft, and jail"—that is, it should attend to and possibly also introduce economic anxiety to the player's act of play.[18] But Castronova goes on to detail the concept even more, arguing that "fun economies" should have "major events and epochs at the macro level."[19] While Castronova provides a comparatively much more detailed consideration of economics than Murray, it is useful to note that he too concludes his argument by stating that it is simply too soon to know if his predictions will bear out or can bear out. He notes that the very act of trying to construct an economy around a notion like "fun" is not something that, to his knowledge, has been attempted so far.[20]

To the extent that the fun economy of hypothetical *El Dorado* is set in opposition to the not-so-fun economy of *World of Poverty*, it is possible to make several inferences about the relevance of poverty—understood generally—to fun economies. Whether or not these inferences speak to the works of "human import" created by "more sophisticated developers" is a matter that will be set aside for the moment. As presented, the fun economy is managed to provide possibilities of punishment and reward. That is to say, it appears to operate with baked-in notions of players ascending and descending as economic entities in their course of play. Castronova is not writing to detail what these changes may portend for the player's experience—other than that they are "fun"—but his comments do suggest that such changes would be a key or prime feature of the act of play. This notion is not distinct from Murray's comments on simulation, but it does suggest that "economic security" might be conceptualized as not just one of several "overlapping states of mind" for the player: rather, the subject might be considered fundamental to play itself in such environments.

This line of reasoning emerges under distinct concerns in Nick Dyer-Witheford and Greig de Peuter's *Games of Empire: Global Capitalism and Video Games*. In that text, the concept of poverty emerges a number of times, and in contexts that are sometimes similar to and sometimes distinctive from those that have been addressed so far. For example, there are instances in the text in which poverty is deployed in a list of non-specific social ills and also in such a way that it is associated with the writing of a specific academic source: in this case the work of Mike Davis via Negri.[21] Dyer-Witheford and de Peuter attend to the ways in which "modern capitalist urbanization combines gated communities, glittering towers of finance, and glamorous playgrounds of consumption with poverty, racialized segregation, gang activity, and militarized policing."[22] The notion is also associated with the work of David Harvey. Elsewhere, this trend continues with the authors addressing poverty generally in the context of social systems that intentionally yoke it with particular manifestations of wealth: that is, they envision "imperial cityscapes, where spaces of wealth and poverty, privilege and depression, are inscribed along the lines of neoaparthides."[23] Late in the text, the authors begin to move toward a more specific conversation on poverty when they introduce the concept of "global poverty" and address its relevance to titles associated with "an increasingly crowded game subfield."[24] However, the term is never detailed, though it hangs as a concept with supposed relevance to the game *3rd World Farmer*.[25]

Arguably, *Games of Empire*'s more significant and distinctive commentary on poverty emerges fairly early on in the text when the authors create a distinction between "poverty" and "virtual poverty."[26] The distinction is introduced in their commentary on *Second Life*. While commenting on the economic significance of the game's currency—Linden Dollars—the authors note that real fortunes have been made by players willing to infuse large sums of money into their gameplay experiences. These economic developments create "income disparities" between players that enable a 20 percent minority to enjoy fantastic riches while "the rest languish in virtual poverty." They then note that "virtual poverty is of course not the same as actual poverty." They base this distinction on the player's contexts for play, noting

> Playing *Second Life* requires a computer and a broadband connection, which in itself limits access to the upper percentiles of global wealth. … Inhabitants of *Second Life* are, in other words, class-divided, property-owning, commodity-exchanging, currency-trading, networking, energy-consuming subjects of a comprehensively capitalist order.[27]

While this moment is of little note in the context of the authors' larger argument, it represents a conceptual leap in the field, even if this leap has yet to be exploited by subsequent commentary. Virtual poverty carries assumptions about the player in his or her act of play that precede and coincide with the act of playing. This tension is anticipated in Murray and Castronova, but the idea that it might be used to assign value to the player and his or her acts of play is only a tacit possibility in those arguments. Virtual poverty becomes something of a mockery of actual poverty in the hands of Dyer-Witheford and de Peuter, to the extent that the players are enacting suffering in gameplay experiences that likely do not comport with their lived experiences. However, even as the assertion is made, the issues of definition persist: surely people who have experienced poverty do or have played *Second Life*, as well as other games that involve conceptions of poverty. How might their experiences be reconciled to virtual poverty, or—more importantly—how might virtual poverty be detailed in ways that make it useful for addressing the experiences of such players?

Virtual Poverty and Congruence

To date, the subject of "virtual poverty" has attracted limited but noteworthy attention from the academic community. Such work—along with related commentary on the relevance of identity-formation to the player's act of play—has arrived at a critical juncture for game studies. A broad strokes consideration of the field and its leading lights suggests the past two decades can be characterized by an ongoing consideration of the videogame form and its possible functions. Throughout this period, there has been a steady stream of commentary concerned with the implications of such functions for the player: for example, the interminable debate concerning possible relationships between the player's act of play and acts of physical violence. However, in the last decade, there has been expanding interest in questions bearing on issues of access and representation and the significance of these subjects beyond the immediacy of the gameplay experience. This success with which much of the work has charted novel ground for addressing the relevance of videogames to expanding constituencies is now itself a subject of inquiry. It raises new questions about empathy and demographics, and it also returns to related and ancient questions about humanity itself: that is, to questions about our binding aspirations and anxieties. In short, the moment is one in which game studies is presenting itself as a mature academic discipline, ready to contribute on its own terms to the academy's age-old debates.

Work associated with such development can be found in Alexander R. Galloway's "Social Realism in Games" (2004). Galloway introduces the concept of "congruence," which he uses to specify conditions in which the player's acts of play resonate with the player's socioeconomic conditions.[28] As presented, the term contributes to Galloway's larger effort to call for games with increased sensitivities to the challenging cultural conditions that are, from Galloway's perspective, left unaddressed by many titles produced before the twenty-first century. While Galloway's larger argument is disputed in a later portion of this book, "congruence" is a very useful concept for addressing Dyer-Witheford and de Peuter's comments on the divide between poverty and virtual poverty. It allows one to specify virtual poverty as something other than a mimicry or mockery of poverty and to conceptualize it instead as a phenomenon that emerges in relationship to the extent to which in-game income distributions align with or can be divorced from the lived experiences of players in their acts of play.

The association of virtual poverty with congruence underscores the need for poverty to be conceptualized with respect to particularized subjects. In the last decade, several noteworthy arguments have emerged that have addressed such subjects with various levels of specificity, and such work has prepared the field for our common moment, one in which fine-tuned conceptions of poverty might be applied to the player's acts of play to illuminate its relevance to gaming communities. Kocurek's *Coin-Operated Americans: Rebooting Boyhood in the Video Game Arcade* (2015) is one such text. While poverty is not a named concept in that work, the author provides a detailed account of the economic and industrial conditions of play, extending from the nineteenth century to the present. The account is one that associates economic activity around the player's act of play in the early coin-operated entertainment industry and the twentieth-century video arcade scene with specific forms of anxiety sourced to "moral reformers."[29] Kocurek deploys the term a number of times in her argument to name and usually shame those whose "social standards reflect existent norms rather than the emergent values of a society in transition."[30] For Kocurek, game playing tends to exist in opposition to such types. Her position is perhaps best expressed as follows:

> Moral reformers' discomfort with the hours that teens spent playing video games reflects uneasiness with the implications of these broader cultural and economic shifts. Children were not growing up with negative moral values so much as they were being brought up as natives of the new economy; adults who had grown up in an era of company men, Fordist production, and savings accounts were watching the young grow up in an age of rapid-fire career changes, flexible accumulation, and easy credit. The intense competition of the arcade, filled with 8-bit violence and the enticement to spend this week's allowance and next week's all in one go, seemed decidedly unwholesome.[31]

In the context of virtual poverty and congruence, the panic of Kocurek's moral reformers extends from the notion that the act of play itself is impoverishing: that is to say, accessing experiences of virtual poverty comes with the threat of actual economic ruination for some members of society.

As was the case with "virtual poverty," one of the benefits and challenges of the phrase "moral reformers" is the associated notion that the lived experience of game players may also involve such concerns—that is, the division between players and moral reformers might be conceived of as a binary, but it is equally reasonable to hold the players may have such or related beliefs about the economic consequences of play even as they play. This does not invalidate the state of mind Kocurek details, but it does allow for such concerns to break into the actual gamed space of play, where it may or may not be addressed by the act of play. In this context, Galloway's notion of congruence takes on additional urgency to the extent that games may emerge with gameplay experiences that are receptive to the economic anxieties of moral reformers. Indeed, this is exactly one of the major contributions of Kocurek's work, which seeks to chart how the videogame arcade responded to various social pressures on play in ways that facilitated the growth and expansion of the industry.

Such work has an unexplored bearing on what Kocurek terms the cultural identity of the video gamer, and in particular with notions of how this identity is reconciled with notions of financial responsibility through the act of play—most notably through competitive acts.[32] She identifies and follows the economic development of the gamer across several decades and renders a noteworthy image of the gamer as a multifaceted subject contextualized by the particular growth and development of the gaming industry. Kocurek's characterization of the cultural identity of video gamer as an identity beset by the economic anxieties of moral reformers has implications for play that are as significant as Dyer-Witheford and de Peuter's conception of virtual poverty: it introduces and suggests a path for future scholarship with an explicit investment in notions of economic status. Under Kocurek's scheme, the gamer may or may not be poor, but the ever-present threat of wasted resources hangs over the gamer's acts of play. Under Dyer-Witheford and De Peuter's scheme, the player's enactment of poverty hangs as an open question for how the act of play might be associated if not reconciled with actual poverty. Both views are united by a concern with poverty—and both are troubled by the notion that poverty as such lacks definition within the field. However, before pursuing the pathways for analysis that are suggested under the reasoning of authors like Kocurek, Dyer-Witheford, and de Peuter, it is important to recognize that game studies has accrued and promulgated certain rhetorical tropes for broaching and exploring economic anxieties. A review of such patterning reveals key moments in the field's development over the past two decades, and an understanding of these moments can be used to contextualize much of the work ahead.

Authoritative Dispatches from the Field

Janet Murray's *Hamlet on the Holodeck: The Future of Narrative in Cyberspace* can serve as a point of departure for such analysis, under the observation that the document's attention to economics as it relates to the player's act of play never rises above the level of general speculation. This is not a shortcoming of the work. The title operates under a thesis that does not directly bear on economics: that is, Murray's attention is trained on the notion that "computation offers a powerful new set of expressive affordances for the ancient human activity of storytelling."[33] However, along the way there are momentary asides when the author notes in passing a relationship between economics and videogames. For example, she observes that "the technical and economic cultivation of this fertile new medium of communication has led to several new varieties of narrative entertainment" Later, and as noted already, she writes that "economic and social forces may never move the established game industry far past the lucrative shoot-'em-ups and puzzle mazes."[34] And, as seen, even later she recognizes the limitations of such observations, noting that "we cannot yet predict the economics of the television-internet merger." When these comments are offered, they are offered without explicit or implicit associations to economic scholarship. This too is not a shortcoming of the text, which has its own very reasonable focus, but it is a feature of Murray's discourse, one that is relevant to a number of related efforts in the field.

A distinct approach that successfully links such commentary with economic scholarship is found in Edward Castronova's *Synthetic Worlds: The Business and Culture of Online Games.* With an operational definition of "synthetic worlds" as "crafted places inside computers that are designed to accommodate large numbers of people," Castronova advances a thesis that "synthetic worlds now emerging from the computer game industry ... are becoming an important host of ordinary human affairs."[35] Castronova explicitly frames his argument as a speculative endeavor and offers an extensive and sustained commentary on the economic possibilities of synthetic worlds, most famously perhaps with his commentary on the "fun economy."[36] While speculative, the comments, in contrast to comments from Murray, have the added authority of Castronova's credentialing as an economist, though the limits of that authority are significant and self-avowed—illuminated by the author, who describes himself as an economist pushing into "a realm that's growing faster than [he] can examine it." In terms of the academic contexts for such statements, Castronova appeals to a remarkably small and select body of criticism, most notably to works from James Buchanan and Bruno Frey, which address the relationship between happiness and wealth. In their contexts, such efforts to link traditional economic scholarship to the "realm that is growing faster than [Castronova] can examine it"[37] are certainly modest, but they are to be valued nevertheless to the extent that they stand as early evidence of an effort to use scholarship on economic matters to address the player's act of play.

A related effort that demonstrates a similar interest in select associations with economic scholarship can be found in Ian Bogost's *Persuasive Games: The Expressive Power of Videogames.* Bogost's "analysis of the way videogames mount arguments and influence players" unfolds in the defense of the notion that "videogames open a new domain for persuasion, thanks to their core representational mode, procedurality."[38] In comparison to the work of Murray and Castronova, *Persuasive Games* does not present itself as a speculative effort—at least, not explicitly. This is evident from the very beginning, where Bogost, unlike Murray and Castronova, does not self-identify as an academic working at the margins of a traditional field, but rather as a figure with apparently extraordinary expertise, touching on fields as wide-ranging as videogames development, videogame scholarship, children's culture, rhetoric, politics, advertising, and pedagogy. In this context, Bogost makes numerous, general comments on economic matters, and it is often the case that he ties these comments to scholarship with footnotes. Generally, his practice with such referencing is summative and affirmative. That is, he paraphrases without qualification. This is the case with his use of Deirdre McCloskey and Gerard R. Butters. This is also the case with what is arguably his most detailed reflection on economic matters and their bearing on this chosen subject of inquiry: that is, Bogost attends to the disastrous consequences of laissez-faire economics in Britain as a cautionary example of how "philosophies can act as logics for political thought and action"[39] and "an example of a procedural system that underwrites political, economic, and daily practice."

While academic referencing is somewhat more extensive in Bogost's text than in Castronova's, the two documents are united in what amount to a fairly uncomplicated use of scholarship on economics: cited sources are simply presented as authoritative dispatches from the field, and not as, themselves, speculative efforts that exist in the context of competing views and field-specific assumptions. As was the case with Murray's general comments, this shared feature of the writing is not a shortcoming, as the scope of neither text suggests that either author is aiming for this level of complexity. However, as the field moved into and out of the Great Recession (2007–2009) scholarship with an ear for the many and competing voices that contribute to the social science of economics began to emerge. This is also the same moment when the concept of poverty became significant to game studies. Nick Dyer-Witheford and Greig de Peuter's *Games of Empire: Global Capitalism and Video Games* is a document that illuminates that moment. At the level of thesis, the work holds to the notion that "video games are a paradigmatic media of empire – planetary, militarized hypercapitalism – and of some of the forces presently challenging it."[40] Dyer-Witheford and de Peuter situate their effort and their argument in the context of a compelling list of academic entities, some of which convey field-specific perspectives: for example, the Faculty of Information and Media Studies at the University of Western Ontario, the School of Communication at Simon Frasier University, and students in political economy classes in the communications studies department at Wilfrid Laurier University. As was the case with Castronova and Bogost, the context here is significant, at least in terms of the subsequent discussion of economic matters, speculative or otherwise: it leads to reasonable questions about the authors' familiarity with the social science of economics. As was the case with Castronova, and Bogost, the subject emerges quite frequently in the document, and at least in contrast to Murray, Castronova, and Bogost, it is more often the case that the subject is discussed in the immediate context of a cited source. A full listing is probably not needed here to underscore how the text is distinct from previous works, but the contributions from Michael Hardt and Antonio Negri, David Harvey, Carlo Vercellone, Jennifer Johns, Mary Jane Irwin, Alexander Galloway, Michel Foucault, Julian Dibbell, John Beverly, and David Houston are addressed. Importantly, while some of these sources are themselves economists (e.g., Jennifer Johns), others like David Harvey and Michel Foucault represent a spectrum of theoretical thought on economic matters, while others, like Alexander Galloway, represent game studies scholars approaching economic questions in their criticism. In the context of Murray, Castronova, and Bogost, Dyer-Witheford and de Peuter's approach represents a rather sudden and dramatic shift into literature on or surrounding economic matters. This is what a broadening of the field looks like.

However, a distinction in scope is not necessarily the same as a distinction in use, but it is the case that Dyer-Witheford and de Peuter can be described as using these sources in ways that vary from Castronova and Bogost. Scholarship on economic matters tends to be quoted, not paraphrased, in *Games of Empire*, and such quotes are often presented in the immediate context of other quoted sources for the purpose of constructing a warrant—that is, in an effort to explore the relevance of a controlling claim or purpose in the writing. Without implying that quotations are rhetorically superior or inferior to paraphrases, one effect of the discourse is to literally broaden the range of voices represented in the text, to convey the sense of a shared conversation on the matter at hand. The impact of this practice on the reader is essentially distinct from the experience of reading *Synthetic Worlds* or *Persuasive Games*. Arguably, it represents a rhetorical shift as significant for scholarship on the relevance of economics to the player's act of play as the shift we witnessed from pure speculation to limited academic engagement between *Hamlet on the Holodeck* and *Synthetic Worlds*.

Interestingly, the context for this shift does not appear to be unresolved questions or theoretical possibilities found in the identified work from Murray, Castronova, or Bogost. Neither *Hamlet on the Holodeck* nor *Synthetic Worlds* is referenced in the document, and *Persuasive Games* has an extremely limited presence. Rather, the shift appears to be compelled by a collection of related economic conditions we now call the Global Great Recession: The authors, writing during that recession, explain:

> In 2008-9 a compounding series of crises shook the market system, from subprime crisis to stock market plunge to credit crunch to full-bore recession. Amid the ongoing convulsions, however, global capitalism has one consolation left for its increasingly desperate subjects ... you can always stay home (if you still have one) and play a video game.[41]

Arguably, to the extent that *Games of Empire* finds its exigence for analysis in cultural conditions that involve but certainly exceed matters of "computation," "synthetic worlds," and "game-specific forms of discourse," it emerges from and speaks to intersecting academic concerns. In terms of economics, the document's rhetoric reveals an effort to establish an interpretive scheme with and through such concerns—rather than an effort to speculate at the expense of such concerns.

To the extent that *Hamlet on the Holodeck*, *Synthetic Worlds*, *Persuasive Games*, and *Games of Empire* indicate discursive possibilities for considering the relevance of economics to the player's act of play, such possibilities should be considered in the broader context of each work's stated goals and intended audiences. There is no reason, for example, to argue that *Games of Empire* is somehow superior to *Persuasive Games* or that notions of superiority or inferiority between any of these texts should be pursued based on the observations in this chapter. Rather, the larger point is that the discursive possibilities themselves stand ready for future consideration and clarification, to be adapted or otherwise made useful for scholars working to recognize, establish, or articulate connections between game studies and the broader academy. For example, do we have examples of other scholarship from before the Global Great Recession that engages with social issues that were significant to the collapse? How were game studies scholars considering such subjects in the lead up to the calamity, and how have they gone on to talk about it since?

Specifying Poverty for Future Game Studies Investigations

One explanation for why general characterizations of poverty tend to emerge in lists or close associations with paired concerns in game studies scholarship is because the concept itself is extremely context-dependent.

Merriam-Webster defines the term as "the state of one who lacks a usual or socially acceptable amount of money or material possessions."[42] *The Encyclopedia Britannica* uses this same definition,[43] and [44] uses an essentially similar definition, "the state or condition of having little or no money, goods, or means of support." The first two definitions' use of "usual or socially acceptable" underscores the necessity of poverty emerging from a context within which such details are discernible. As deployed in *Woke Gaming*, it is not at all clear how discernible those details may or may not be. For example, what are the dimensions of poverty understood as such in *Grand Theft Auto: San Andreas*? How are individuals, regions, zones, and other aspects of play represented in ways that convey notions of relative lack with respect to notions of usual or socially acceptable amounts? The fact that there is not an answer is not a shortcoming of the text or of the essays that make use of the term—quite to the contrary: the collection foregrounds critical possibilities that invite specification. The clumping together of poverty with crime, sexism, and racism in *Woke Gaming* is of course quite reasonable, given what is known about the deleterious effects of poverty on communities. However, the lumping together itself does not provide a reasonable path for determining notions of what is or is not usual in terms of the acquisition of meaningful materials.

An initial challenge, then, for commentary on the representation of poverty in videogames is the challenge of ascertaining a game-specific scheme for recognizing and defining poverty. Gaming histories, such as those composed by Kocurek and Newman, are generally attentive to specific contexts for play—that is, the arcade or the home console—and also suggest pathways for inquiry that are specific to certain decades: both have a special focus on the 1970s and 1980s. Such work is instructive here, as it works against formalist notions that "videogames" can be meaningfully conceptualized as a unified media category. The sociological and historical forces—and the economic forces—bearing on the player's acts of play are temporally unique, even when their influence on gameplay persists across years and possibly decades. Kocurek and Newman make the wise decision to establish the economic conditions of play relevant to the emergence of the arcade and the home console before launching into their detailed commentaries on gameplay experiences that emerged from those contexts.

Such and related works have established useful boundaries for considering games, those who play games, and the intersection of these subjects. The argument that follows takes a special interest in that final subject: the intersection of game player and game. I have used and will use the phrase "the player's act of play" to reference such intersections. The phrase is deployed for its capacity to foreground the act of play over the subjects of the player and the played (i.e., the game). While the act of play is necessarily contextualized by these subjects, the act of play can be distinguished from both in at least two significant ways. First, the act represents a melding of in-game opportunities for play with the unique play position and perspectives of the player. The opportunity for play may or may not be grounded in a fun economy and may or may not facilitate congruence—but it marks an instance of convergence between the player and that which is played, which can be located in time and associated with other such moments. In the abstract, it is true that this conception establishes only the loosest of boundaries for analysis—literally the player and the game. However, the player's act of play might be specified so that it is bound by additional concerns. With respect to the subject of this book, the relevant concerns will be poverty or will be related to notions relevant to various conceptions of poverty.

In the established literature, there is no particular rationale for the various games, imaginary or real, that scholars have selected to demonstrate their conceptions of poverty or its relevance to gameplay. It is true that *Second Life* and *The Sims* emerge in a number of examples, but these examples do not contain rationales for why these games might be particularly good examples out of any number of other examples. As game studies has yet to chart such a course, this argument now encounters the challenge of how to defend a selection of titles for analysis. That work can begin with the recognition that there is an established and growing body of scholarship that anticipates answers to the kinds of observations that are promised under the above consideration of the player's acts of play. *Woke Gaming* might be singled out here as one such work, to the extent that it anticipates and calls for games to be put to work in the service of social justice—a concern that raises meaningful questions about how, when, why, and under what conditions the player's act of play could be aligned with a progressive agenda.

The Player's Act of Play: Slumming as Transmedia Context

As a subject of academic interest, the videogame player's act of play can be traced to the turn of the century and is arguably associated with a number of twentieth-century publications. However, such work took on a sudden depth and remarkable breadth with the rise of self-described "middle state" commentary on games and gamers in our century's second decade. As defined by Jason Hawreliak, the middle state publication is a publication that seeks to provide "the timeliness and succinctness of a blog, while retaining the rigor and context of a conventional journal article."[45] Middle state publications include, but are not limited to, *Critical Distance* (2009–), *First Person Scholar* (2012–), *Not Your Mama's Gamer* (2012–), and *Game Studies 101* (2015–). In their various mission statements, many of these publications underscore the notion that diverse perspectives stand to energize and/or enlighten the field. For example, *First Person Scholar*'s statement reads in part: "We are looking for unique and diverse perspectives that may be underrepresented in games writing, as well as those that exist between the more industry-driven journalistic view and the more traditional academic position. This means that we are especially interested in submissions from people of color, queer folks, women, and non-binary individuals." *Critical Distance* expresses a desire "to promote the works and voices of those not already served by the mainstream. We believe those outside the main body of the conversation can have as much if not more to contribute as an established critic."[46]

A sense of how the middle state's concerns translated into academic monographs can be ascertained from a consideration of the previously considered *Coin-Operated Americans: Rebooting Boyhood at the Video Game Arcade* and *Atari Age: The Emergence of Video Games in America*. The works recognize the significance of identity to the player's acts of play in modern gaming markets. Kocurek argues that conceptions of the player as a "video gamer" developed during the 1970s, "video gaming's first decade." Newman also expresses an interest in emergent notions of "gamers" from the 1970s. However, unlike Kocurek, the primary subject of Newman's monograph is not video gamers per se, but, rather, the objects that facilitates their leisure. He offers "a new media history of video games, charting their emergence in the United States during their first decade of public, commercial availability, beginning around 1972."[47] A common notion in both works is that new media associated with gaming and the cultural identity of video gamers are associated with long-standing, North American, middle-class status anxieties about players wasting time while playing.

When Edward Castronova reviews and details the functions of "fun economies," he is both postulating how economic matters might bear on the player's acts of play and also setting out something of a roadmap for future designers: that is, he is working to clarify for latent gameplay features that, in his estimation, facilitate the player's acts of play in successful online environments.[48] When Dyer-Witheford and de Peuter observe the divide between virtual poverty and actual poverty, they too are summoning to mind latent features of play that are supposedly determinative with respect to the player's acts of play. The authors are calling attention to an aspect of play that is likely critical for designers to address in some fashion. Such observations raise questions about the possible nature—or natures—of the player's acts of play: that is, are there economic concerns that exist across gameplay experiences that give a common shape to—or provide common shapes for—the player's act of play? The question calls to mind Murray's concern that market forces might curtail in astounding ways the kinds of games that would emerge for twenty-first-century audiences.

Questions bearing on the supposed nature or natures of videogames might begin with the useful observation that the term itself is only loosely defined within game studies. Famously, Murray, Aarseth, Juul, Castronova, Dyer-Witheford, and de Peuter do not define the term with much success, though there are contextual implications for their related comments, and these can generally be squared with the term as it might be found in any number of popular dictionaries, such as *Merriam-Webster*, which defines the term as "an electronic game in which players control images on a video screen."[49] The inclusion of "player" in the definition underscores the significance of the player's act of play to the videogame form. Michael Z. Newmann has considered this connection and argues that videogames have "emerged without fixed meaning, without a clear identity, without a commonly shared understanding of their cultural status."[50] He also makes the useful observation that "technologies" (such as those associated with videogames) "pass through a period of interpretive flexibility, as different social groups adapt them for divergent purposes, before a process of closure establishes a clearer identity, marking some uses dominant while others before more marginal and are cast aside."[51] Given that successive waves of game studies scholarship have been oftentimes at odds over the question of how and for what purposes videogames are used, it strikes me that the medium may still very much be in a state of "interpretive flexibility," one in which it has a set of recognizable meanings with open-ended significance to the form and our understanding of its boundaries. In this context, questions of economic essentialism become decidedly less interesting than questions of economic possibilities—that is, what economic concerns might be associated with the player's acts of play, and to what extent are such concerns useful for understanding the acts themselves. This notion is latent in Alexander Galloway's comments on congruence and also in Castronova's conception of the fun economy—to the extent that both underscore the significance of crafting a gameplay experience that will resonate with a certain type or certain types of players.

To the extent that a "controlling" player plays with established as well as developing conceptions of poverty, videogames might be explored for their capacities to facilitate player's expressions of such conceptions. That is, Castronova's "fun economies" are designed for players with assumed or developing economic impulses, and those impulses might be entertained in, as Dyer-Witheford and de Peuter argue, a videogame like *Second Life*.[52] Galloway's comments on congruence suggest that videogames may be as capable of frustrating such expectations as they are of supporting them—a notion that can be squared without much difficulty with Newmann's conditions of a technology that emerges without a clear identity, but rather develops by assuming identities associated with expanding or dominant ideologies. Taken together, these concerns suggest one productive path forward for the analysis at hand is to begin with questions of how poverty might be conceptualized in transmedia entertainments that both precede and continue to inform the videogame industry. One such history can be located in the subject of "slumming."

With respect to broad conceptions of poverty, early—and admittedly limited—work moving in this direction has appeared on the subject of "slumming" and its relevance to the player's act of play. Modern conceptions of slumming emerged during the same period when the coin-operated entertainment industry appeared. As addressed by Eveline Dürr and Rivke Jaffe, slumming emerged as a tourist experience in Victorian England, where "affluent nineteenth-century 'adventurers' … would leave their comfortable, elite spaces to explore underprivileged urban districts."[53] This practice, they explain, "spread to cities in the USA, where slumming included trips to so-called 'ethnic' and 'exotic' neighborhoods, such as 'Little Italy' and 'China Town.'" According to Igor Kristić, the period was marked by middle-class audiences and readerships fascination with "fiction and non-fiction stories from the 'urban underworld,'" as produced in "journalistic sketches, essayistic travelogues, theatrical plays [and] naturalistic novels about life, crime and social misery in the slums."[54] Kristić notes that, by the turn of the century, "[m]agic lantern 'slum shows'" began to appear, "projecting … images of slums" that had been circulating in prose throughout the nineteenth century to new, international audiences.[55] Ingrid Stigsdotter observes that during the twentieth century, the related phenomenon of "cinematic slumming" took shape, which involved elite, art-house audiences consuming films about the "lower classes [generally] from countries other than their own."[56] Stigsdotter argues that early reactions to "the neorealist movement in Italy in the early postwar period"[57]are emblematic of such tastes to the extent that the movement initially found much larger viewerships abroad than at home.

Given the generous historical footprint and international significance of "slumming," "slum shows," and "cinematic slumming" in the nineteenth and twentieth centuries, this transmedia phenomenon resists simple summation. However, it is reasonable to associate it with a particular act: that is, affluent audiences pursuing exoticized representations of the poor and impoverished from an appreciable remove that was either literal or figurative. In terms of game studies, the notion that these kinds of pursuits are relevant to the player's act of play appears in the popular press as early as 2005. That summer, the website *PopMatters* published Michael Stephen's "Safe Danger and Virtual Slumming." There, Stephen considers "the proliferation of entertainment products," for example, "video games, movies [and] T.V.," that "allow middle-class consumers to traffic in the inner city without leaving the culs-de-sac" and argues that "as digital media achieves more detailed simulations of reality … the quest for thrills mutates into a desire, not just to see bigger and better explosions, but to cross class and racial boundaries and experience other lifestyles."[58] Apparently unaware of the history of "slumming" and "slum tourism," Stephen coins the phrase "ghetto tourism" to describe this "desire."[59]

Prior to 2005, monographs now associated with game studies provide some limited awareness of the essential conditions of slum tourism, if not slum tourism itself, and their relevance to videogames. For example, Murray (1997) briefly considers Baudrillard's concept of "hyperreality"—that is, the preference for a representation over the thing the representation represents, with the example from Umberto Eco of Main Street USA at Disney World.[60] Murray recognizes that the hyperreal is seductive because it presents an opportunity to overlook the broader cultural consequences of the represented (303–04). A related concern can be located in Galloway's "Social Realism in Gaming." Galloway's concluding call for a "social realist" aesthetic in gaming modeled on the Italian neorealist movement indicates, if nothing else, an opportunity for videogames to represent the underprivileged in ways that compel anti-fascist action.[61] Taken together, then, Murray and Galloway convey a general sense that the player's act of play carries an implicit threat for the poor: it promises an opportunity to overlook the broader social implications of the represented. In the case of Murray, it would be an overstatement to indicate that this opportunity rises to the level of a major critical concern. Nevertheless, as context for Stephen's "ghetto tourism," her comments qualify Stephen's assertion that the quest for such "thrills" is simply predicated on "more detailed simulations of reality" and, instead, is more accurately understood as being predicated on the curated experience that is offered to the viewer within "simulated reality." The history of slum tourism indicates select cultural conditions with contextual significance of such curation: middle- and upper-class interest in ogling a curious poor in an exoticized habitat—from an arm's length.

The notion that the player's acts of play can be associated with slumming and conceptions of slumming takes my argument to its next crucial divide: just as videogame formalism must be rejected in favor of contextualized and qualified explorations of the medium, so too it is necessary to abandon the notion that the player's acts of play might be conceptualized to a point of atomistic certainty. Rather, the concept is useful for analysis when, and perhaps only when, it is particularized through association: when associated with the cultural phenomenon of slumming, the player's acts of play can be considered for how they shed light on slumming itself. At the same time, the concept of slumming stands poised to further illuminate conceptions of the player's acts of play.

The Intersection of Player and Played: Slumming in *Skyrim*

The limited nature of scholarship on poverty and its relevance to videogames poses a serious challenge for actual analysis—namely, where and how does one begin to pursue such concerns? One promising point of entry for such work is scholarship on gaming that offers conceptions of economic patterns and their relevance to play. Ideally, for the work at hand, such arguments might be productively associated with notions of poverty as well as notions of slumming. One such work is offered by David M. Higgins, who writes,

> many single-player video games model economic systems that embody contemporary capitalism's dreams of optimum social and economic expression. *Skyrim*, for example, presents a world where all objects, including living souls, can be integrated into an endless cycle of commodity production and trade.[62]

The claim calls out for specification and elaboration. For example, the notion that "many single-player games model economic systems that embody contemporary capitalism's dreams of optimum social and economic expression" is striking. Higgins does not establish a foundation for understanding the origins or supposed agenda for "contemporary capitalism's dreams of optimum social and economic expression." Nevertheless, he does go on to imply that such a model can be located in *Skyrim*—under the notion that the game "presents a world where all objects, including living souls, can be integrated into an endless cycle of commodity production and trade." However, that is not a notion that is actually supported by *Skyrim* gameplay. To be sure, there are many "objects" the player can acquire, produce, and trade—but, no, that is not true of "all objects" in the game, a notion affirmed by any number of tables, chairs, doors, and encampment objects that appear in the course of play. However, even if the claim was true, the notion that such production and trade enact an "endless cycle" would also be contestable—this is because *Skyrim* features production and trade but it is of course not delimited by such acts.

If this response to Higgins strikes the ear as too strident, too literal, then the ear is hearing correctly. The point is not to simply dismiss Higgins' excellent commentary, but, rather, to open space for what is an arguably more detailed line of analysis that might shed light on the shape of *Skyrim*'s noteworthy investments in capitalist systems, which include slums. As Mike Piero and Marc A. Ouellette note, *Skyrim* is an "exemplary gameworld" for critical analysis on the basis of its long-standing and persistent popularity with players and the "complex space" for play it offers across an ever-broadening range of gameplay devices.[63] With respect to the argument at hand, one early effort to detail the game's many and varied economic systems is offered by Kevin and Brent Moberly. They note that

Skyrim's "mixture of industrial and feudal economic traditions are presented as parallel, interchangeable, and equally as ancient (or modern)."[64] This particularity of the game's sites of production and marketplaces indicates that while the title may or may not embody contemporary capitalism's dreams of optimum social and economic expression, such embodiment is necessarily exotic with respect to the economic context of the player's act of play—which is assumedly neither essential feudal nor industrial, nor a likely transposition of these two traditions. From this, it can be concluded that the game indicates the possibility of economic difference by overlooking the essential social conditions that would normally preclude such difference. This "overlooking," it can be argued, is foundational to the player's act of play in *Skyrim*. Arguments considered so far from Castronova, Galloway, and Dyer-Witheford and de Peuter would all suggest that this system—odd as it may be—is grounded in a key assumption or set of assumptions: namely, that *Skyrim*'s economic systems make a certain sense to a certain kind of player—the kind of player who will derive some sense of enjoyment from what is represented and (to draw from Murray) from what is obscured by the game's anachronistic, postmodern economic systems.

An effort to build on the work of Moberly and Moberly can begin with the notion that the game's market opportunities overlook the possibility of economic difference in another, equally fascinating way. Generally, the game offers players the possibility to interact with a range of merchants across Skyrim's major and minor dwellings. Game player resources such as *The Elder Scrolls Wiki* and *The Elder Scrolls Skyrim: Special Edition Wiki* organize these merchants under the categories of Apothecaries, Blacksmiths, Fences, General, Innkeepers, Jewelers, and Spell merchants. While each merchant's objects on hand for sale may vary from one region to the next and can also be affected by the player's advancement through the game itself, the overwhelming trend across all merchant classes is for merchants to have access to a set amount of gold for bartering. Changes to this pattern depend primarily on the player's act of play and the extent to which the player has invested points in a "speech" attribute, which under certain conditions can impact the financial resources of select merchants. Under this system, the game overlooks the likely economic conditions of its merchants on two levels: first at the level of social situation, for example, their immediate markets have apparently no impact on their financial situation, and second at the level of player-interaction when the economic system is literally reorganized to accommodate certain forms of player investment (e.g., in the speech attribute). In this way the game is overlooking the essential economic conditions that prefigure production and exchange and therein lies its seduction.

These factors serve as a meaningful context for the game's primary, explicitly referenced "slum"—the Gray Quarter in Windhelm. The Gray Quarter is home to Windhelm's displaced Dark Elf, or "Dunmer," population, which is, at the moment of the player character's arrival, impoverished and under threat of racial violence from Windhelm's ethnic founders. While the player's interactions with the Gray Quarter inhabitants will vary depending upon the player's own chosen race, if the player character is any race other than Dunmer, there is a strong possibility that the player will be quickly associated with the concept of slumming by the local Malthyr Elenil, who asks, "Come slumming to the Gray Quarter, have you?" While Elenil's comments will ultimately depend on a number of possible narrative developments that pre-date the player's arrival in the Gray Quarter, if Elenil is pressed about Dunmer life in the quarter and Windhelm, he indicates that the Dark Elf population is a refugee population that has settled in Windhelm and has been under constant racial threat since their arrival and that the squalor of their daily lives is being actively ignored by the security and political classes in the city.

In terms of the notions of "overlooking" and "the curious poor," it can be noted that while the Gray Quarter is identified as a slum in extreme duress, its merchants are on an equal economic footing with all the other merchants in *Skyrim*. For example, Ambarys Rendar is the Innkeeper in The Gray Quarter. In *Skyrim*, all Innkeepers have initial access to 100 or 50 gold, with the majority having access to 100 gold. Rendar has access to 100 gold, despite the stated social conditions of the Gray Quarter. The other merchant in the Gray Quarter, Aval Atheron, runs a marketplace stall and sells "general items." General merchants in *Skyrim* universally have access to 750 gold, regardless of their location, and Atheron has this amount of money on hand for bartering. These characters enjoy economic conditions that undermine notions of individuality, but they also enforce notions that the player's act of play is occurring in a set and stable economic environment, the conditions of which supersede the cultural conditions of any one or several locations.

Rendar and Atheron's participation in *Skyrim*'s remarkably stable Innkeeper and General Merchant economies undercuts the notion that the Gray Quarter is a region that is experiencing serious economic consequences and conveys a sense that the title's refugee population does not have an economic foundation for its complaints of racial hatred and abuse. This notion can be extended to either merchant's available goods, which are essentially indistinguishable from the goods sold by similar merchants at other locations in the game. In terms of *Skyrim*'s participation in the long history of "slum tourism" and "slumming" experiences, it can be noted that the title exoticizes its slum dwellers by overlooking evidence of their economic plight. However, it is also true that such overlooking is relevant to all merchants at all locations in *Skyrim*. Their finances in common suggest that each merchant operates outside of the cultural or geographic pressures of his or her shop and instead operates under an overarching economic determination that operates without attention to such pressures. As a result, *Skyrim*'s market logic establishes an essentially exotic economic experience, one that is no more particular to the slum than it is to any other region in the game. The notion seems significant given that the region's bloody civil war is context for the player's act of play, and while the game speaks to and represents the social and cultural realities of that war, it appears to have no appreciable impact on the various economies represented in *Skyrim*.

Skyrim's merchants' holdings-in-common establish a fantasy for play that mimics economic markets but overlooks the foundational forces that impact such markets. To the extent that the long tradition of slum tourism has included middle-class audiences regarding the impoverished outside of essential economic realities, *Skyrim* can be envisioned as a massive slum-of-sorts, in the tradition of slums featured to and for slum tourists: its economic system, at its base, operates without attention to the social and geographic complications of daily life, while, at the same time, it allows the player (the slum tourist) the fantasy of participating in that economy as if the economy included complex market parameters of acquisition and expenditure. In the context of slum tourism, such fantasy can be associated with the necessary division between the "slum tourist and the slum dweller." The tourist's "adventure" is predicated on, and in some senses defined by, their successful retreat from the "underprivileged districts" to their "elite spaces": that is, the cul-de-sac or its equivalent. But of course, *Skyrim* is simply one game in a vast catalogue of gaming possibilities for players. To simply assume that the game's economic conditions are an extension of the gaming form itself would be a gross miscalculation. However, this analysis offered so far does establish a bounded set of assumptions for future analysis of this title and relatable titles. Whether or not these assumptions are productive remains to be seen.

The Intersection of Player and Played: Thematizing Poverty

As a critical framework, "slumming" functions at the level of characterization. It suggests an essential disposition for the player as well as the game. While rationales for this disposition can be extrapolated from the transmedia relevance of slumming in the nineteenth and twentieth centuries, it is not immediately apparent how it is that slumming can clarify understandings of the player's act of play—that is, of the player's interactions with any given videogame. For example, while one might characterize the economic systems in *Skyrim* as, in whole or in part, being resonate with financial fantasies long associated with slumming, this characterization does not itself necessarily tell us anything specific about the title, other than of course that its systems might be characterized in such a way. In order to prove the critical value of slumming to *Skyrim*, it would be necessary to apply the concept in such a way so as to illuminate something distinctive about the game. To the extent that slumming directs critical attention to the representations of poverty, it draws critical attention to poverty as a meaningful facet of gameplay and leads to the general question of how the concept might be further characterized.

With respect to *Skyrim*, the player's experience of poverty has several distinct facets, which contribute to a larger theme. Evidence of this theme can be found in the player's opportunities to acquire and spend across diverse regions and markets. While it is true that the player's inventory may fluctuate in terms of the player's holdings, and while it is true that some items require very specific or extraordinary efforts to acquire, the inventory's persistence over time conveys a specific ambiance to the player's act of play. This ambiance is deterministic, to the extent that the inventory fluctuates in response to player action, and its persistence conveys a limited context for understanding the instances of play as well as the collective implications of play over time. Poverty is not the qualifying characteristic of this economic framing, but it is part of it, to the extent that the inventory's fluctuation conveys notions of how the states of scarcity or abundance bear on the player's acts of play. To the extent that the experience of poverty compels the player to act in ways that lead to acquisition, poverty is a persistent possibility for the player in his or her act of play. However, the significance of this possibility to the player's acts of play is extremely limited, as poverty might be escaped or avoided at any turn through abundant opportunities for acquisition. In short, for the player poverty is experiential but inconsequential to the player's future economic positioning. The reality of play renders poverty a condition without consequences at least with respect to the player's capacity to develop his or her resources over time. Poverty is punitive only with respect to the moment it is recognized, after which it can be ameliorated through right action that takes advantage of gameplay opportunities for acquisition.

In terms of the merchant classes discussed so far, it can also be concluded that poverty is essentially an abstraction. Merchant holdings replenish without indicating that poverty is a financial possibility for the merchants, other than momentarily. Depleted gold reserve refill, and depleted holds of items of all sorts replenish over time. In this way, poverty's seriousness for the player's acts of play is replicated in the economic systems that overlay merchant interactions. However, a very different conception of poverty emerges when a broader view is taken of the general individuals that appear in *Skyrim*. Unlike the player or the merchants, their economic status is essentially immobile and unchanging. They neither participate in the exchange system of the merchants nor participate in other forms of item exchange with the player. Their lot is to be persistent essentially through all major conditions that transpire over the course of the game. That is, while war and destruction may visit their holdings from time to time, as time persists they neither increase nor decrease in terms of their apparent economic positioning within society. Their assumed finances are as secret as their thoughts. It is true that the player can attempt to pick the pocket of any number of people they encounter, and while those efforts reveal how much money a character may have on hand, the larger connection between that money and the wider world remains mysterious.

The interaction of these three aspects of play constitutes *Skyrim*'s poverty theme or the recurrent notion that the player persists in an economic system with manifold paths away from poverty, while much of the rest of the world lives in a steady state of arbitrary economic stagnation. While it is true that various groupings appear to have distinct levels of economic advantage in *Skyrim*, it is also true that those distinctions are essentially immobile at any and all points during the player's acts of play. Detailed, *Skyrim*'s poverty theme stands ready for potential associations with the player's own economic positioning. For Galloway, a resonance between the poverty theme and the player's economic positioning would be conceptualized in terms of congruence. To the extent that congruence indicates notions of commonality between these subjects, it may be a tool for ascertaining evident degrees of similarity between these subjects. For Galloway, such familiarity is meaningful because, in the context of his writing, he is attempting to justify an essential value for videogames within the area of social criticism. And while that effort is noble and productive, congruence is a very specific goal for game design and one that assumes an intentionality on the part of the game designers that is simply unlikely for designers working on games with mass market and international appeal. This is not to say that congruence is a meaningless concept for considering *Skyrim* and similar titles. On the contrary, it suggests a meaningful value of economic simulations in videogames. However, this value is quite broad and stands ready to be specified—for example, with the concept of slumming—to the extent that slumming is conceptually significant to the player's larger economic positioning (not as a determining feature of that positioning, but as one part of nuanced tapestry). Or, to put it in another way, the concept of congruence has served as a much-needed placeholder concept for more specific associations and descriptions of the economic forces and traditions bearing on the player's acts of play: it has cleared the way for a consideration of poverty as *theme*. In the next three chapters, I will consider how titles with economic representations similar to (or otherwise informative of) those considered so far in *Skyrim* construct a poverty theme or themes. This work will begin with a consideration of several titles from Blizzard Entertainment that collectively demonstrate how a poverty thematic can be extended across various gaming genres and also historically distinct gaming conditions.

Notes

1. Juul, 150–51.
2. Bogost, *Persuasive Games*, chap. 1.
3. Rowlands, 59.
4. Ibid.
5. Skardzius, 181.
6. Ibid.
7. Anderson-Barkley, 264.
8. Gee, 11.
9. Murray, 28.
10. Ibid., 54.
11. Ibid., 243.
12. Ibid., 254.
13. Castronova, 2347.

14. Castronova, 2350.
15. Ibid., 2773.
16. Ibid., 2773.
17. Ibid., 2783.
18. Ibid., 2785.
19. Ibid., 2786.
20. Ibid., 4151.
21. Dyer-Witheford, 154.
22. Ibid., 154.
23. Ibid., 167.
24. Ibid., 201.
25. Ibid., 201.
26. Ibid., 105.
27. Ibid., 106.
28. Galloway
29. Kocurek, 509.
30. Ibid., 509.
31. Ibid., 883.
32. Ibid., 121.
33. Murray., 12.
34. Ibid., 54.
35. Castronova, *Synthetic* 80.
36. Ibid., 2773.
37. Ibid., 61.
38. Bogost., 83.
39. Ibid., 1503.
40. Dyer-Witheford, 167.
41. Ibid., 228.
42. MW online.
43. EB online.
44. Dictionary online.
45. Hawreliak, http://www.firstpersonscholar.com/the-case-for-the-middle-state/
46. *Critical Distance.*
47. Newman, 216.
48. Castronova, 2773.
49. Merriam-Webster online.
50. Newman, 220.
51. Ibid., 229.
52. Dyer-Witheford, 95.
53. Dürr, 114.
54. Kristić, 185.

55. Ibid.
56. Stigsdotter, "British Audiences."
57. Ibid.
58. Decter, Wish.
59. Ibid.
60. Murray, 292.
61. Galloway, "Social Realism."
62. Higgins, Dreams 62.
63. Piero, 1.
64. Moberly.

Bibliography

Bogost, Ian. *Persuasive Games: The Expressive Power of Videogames*. Cambridge, Mass: The MIT Press, 2010. Kindle edition.

Castronova, Edward. *Synthetic Worlds: The Business and Culture of Online Games*. Chicago: University of Chicago Press, 2005. Kindle edition.

Chess, Shira. *Ready Player Two: Women Gamers and Designed Identity*. Minneapolis: University of Minnesota Press, 2017. Kindle edition.

Condis, Megan. *Gaming Masculinity: Trolls, Fake Geeks, and the Gendered Battle for Online Culture*. Minneapolis: University of Minnesota Press, 2018. Kindle edition.

Dyer-Witheford, Nick and de Peuter, Greig. *Games of Empire: Global Capitalism and Video Games*. Minneapolis: University of Minnesota Press, 2009. Kindle edition.

Galloway, Alexander R. "Social Realism in Gaming." *Game Studies: The International Journal of Computer Game* 4, no. 1 (November 2004). http://www.gamestudies.org/0401/galloway/.

Gee, J. P. *Good Video Games + Good Learning: Collected Essays on Video Games, Learning and Literacy*. New York: Peter Lang. 2007.

Geraci, Robert M. *Virtually Sacred: Myth and Meaning in* World of Warcraft *and* Second Life. New York: Oxford University Press, 2014. Kindle edition.

Gray, Kishonna and Leonard, David J. *Woke Gaming: Digital Challenges to Oppression and Social Injustice*. Seattle: University of Washington Press, 2018. Kindle edition.

Hayden, Craig. "The Procedural Rhetorics of Mass Effect: Video Games as Argumentation in International Relations." *International Studies Perspectives* (2017): 175–193.

Jayemanne, Darshana. *Performativity in Art, Literature, and Videogames*. Palgrave Macmillan, 2017. Kindle edition.

Kocurek, Carly A. *Coin-Operated Americans: Rebooting Boyhood at the Video Game Arcade* Minneapolis: University of Minnesota Press, 2015. Kindle edition.

Krstić, Igor. "Remediating the 'Other Half': Planet Slum as Transmedia Project" In *Global Cinematic Cities: New Landscapes of Film and Media*. Edited by Johan Andersson and Lawrence Webb, 178–198. New York Chichester, West Sussex: Columbia University Press, 2016. https://doi.org/10.7312/ande17746-011.

Krobová, T., Moravec, O., & Švelch, J. (2015). Dressing Commander Shepard in pink: Queer playing in a heteronormative game culture. *Cyberpsychology: Journal of Psychosocial Research on Cyberspace, 9*(3), Article 3. https://doi.org/10.5817/CP2015-3-3.

Leonard, D. J. "Not a Hater, Just Keepin' It Real: The Importance of Race- and Gender-Based Game Studies." *Games and Culture* 1 (2006): 83–88.

Newman, Michael Z. *Atari Age: The Emergence of Video Games in America*. Cambridge, Mass: MIT Press, 2017. Kindle edition.

Mukherjee, Souvik. *Video Games and Storytelling: Reading Games and Playing Books*. Palgrave Macmillan, 2015. Kindle edition.

Murray, Janet H. *Hamlet on the Holodeck: The Future of Narrative in Cyberspace*. Free Press, 1997. Kindle edition.

Nichols, Randy. *The Video Game Business*. British Film Institute, 2014.

Pearce, Alyssa Maria. "Exploring Performance of Gendered Identities through Language in *World of Warcraft*." *International Journal of Human–Computer Interaction*, 33:3, (2017) 180–189, https://doi.org/10.1080/10447318.2016.1230965.

Shaw, Adrienne. *Gaming at the Edge: Sexuality and Gender at the Margins of Gamer Culture*. Minneapolis: University of Minnesota Press, 2015. Kindle edition.

Snodgrass, Jeffrey G. "Online virtual worlds as anthropological field sites: Ethnographic methods training via collaborative research of Internet gaming cultures." *Annals of Anthological Practice* 40, no. 2 (November 2016): 134–147.

Stark, David K. "Grand Theft Architecture: Architectural Works in Video Games after E.S.S. Entertainment v. Rockstar Games," Berkeley Technology Law Journal 25, no. 1 (2010): 429–464.

Thabet, Tamer. *Video Game Narrative and Criticism: Playing the Story*. Palgrave, 2015. Kindle edition.

Wark, McKenzie. *Gamer Theory*. Boston: Harvard University Press, 2009. Kindle edition.

Welsh, Timothy J. *Mixed Realism: Videogames and the Violence of Fiction*. Minneapolis: University of Minnesota Press, 2017. Kindle edition.

CHAPTER 2

Relative Poverty and Slumming Simulations

Behavior Scripts and Ethical Imperatives

The concept of thematized gameplay economics (e.g., a "poverty theme") is poised to specify understandings of the player's act of play. Related and productive conceptions of how the player and played intersect have been offered by several scholars working in the field of game studies. A consideration of this work can be used to further detail the promises and potential pitfalls for the work ahead. For example, Marta Fernández Ruiz and David García-Reyes have explored the concept of genre-specific "behavioral scripts" that delimit player action into a narrow band of possibilities—either by excluding gameplay options or by rewarding certain behaviors.[1] With respect to the transmedia concept of slumming, Ruiz and Garcia-Reyes offer their comments in their own transmedia investigation—one that concerns a videogame adaptation of a graphic novel. Key in their findings is the notion that the adaptive process necessitates gameplay actions that affirm select thematic concerns from the source material.

Analytical values for behavioral scripts can be inferred from related work from Marina Krcmar and Drew P. Cingel, who consider the ways in which the game *Fallout 3* deploys a series of moral dilemmas to encourage ethical and also unethical in-game player behavior.[2] While the authors do not link their observations to an overarching thematic gameplay concern, the notion that *Fallout 3* and related Bethesda titles have a gameplay

A. Crowley, *Representations of Poverty in Videogames*,
https://doi.org/10.1007/978-3-031-00144-4_2

investment in scripting behavioral crises underscores the notion that the player's act of play is, or at least can be, laden with action opportunities that encourage the player to navigate action in duel, intersecting contexts—the position from which they reason and also the context of play itself.

Independently, Miguel Sicart and David W. Hill approach this concern from related directions. Sicart recognizes that "ill-defined" ethical problems can be used to generate "compelling, ethical experiences" for games but then adds to that notion the assertion that such experiences "must force players to apply moral thinking to their decision-making process, thereby creating ethical gameplay."[3] A related notion is offed by Hill, who argues more broadly that "the images that constitute virtual environments should be understood as morally evocative" and that they "remind us that (represented people) ought to be beyond our unfettered desires, that we might limit our own actions so as not to do injustice to them."[4] Such notions are generally in keeping with Galloway's general conception of congruence, which the author uses as context to call for a conception of right action in gameplay—that is, a particular conception of anti-fascist action.

Taken together, these passages underline two key notions: the first is that behavioral scripts can affirm both transmedia expectations of genre and also title-specific thematic concerns, and the second is that such scripts are subject to external valuations, such as the broad expectations for play that our outlined by Sicart and Hill. As explored in the previous chapter, slumming simulations like those found in *The Elder Scrolls V: Skyrim* are internally complex—that is, they are multifaceted—and raise meaningful questions about the relevance of economics and economic possibilities to the player's act of play. The nature of this complexity becomes all the more apparent with Higgins' limited assessment of the title's economic systems contrasted by the manifold, intersecting models at play in Moberly and Moberly's consideration of the same game. In the context of this complexity, clarion calls like those offed by Galloway, Sicart, and Hill must contend with the notion that while economic systems in games can be associated with moral valuations, a great deal of critical work is potentially needed to articulate and associate such "behavioral scripting" with a specific value set for a player at play. With respect to the phenomenon of poverty as a part of play, such work might begin by specifying the term so that it becomes a more practical tool for analysis.

Specifying Poverty for Analysis: Relative Poverty

The field of economics can be of some use here, with two specific conceptions of poverty: absolute poverty and relative poverty. Absolute poverty is generally defined as "a condition where household income is below a necessary level to maintain basic living standards (food, shelter, housing)."[5] A related term is "relative poverty," commonly defined as a "condition where household income is a certain percentage below median income."[6] The term's association with notions of median income and percentage determinations valued against median income raises questions about its relevance for a title like *Grand Theft Auto: San Andreas*, where basic living standards are not all necessarily specified in ways that lead to assumptions about median income or percent deviations from that income. However, to the extent that relative income implies a recognition of material wealth distinctions that can be made between locations and characters, it might be used as a basic context for analysis. In terms of *Grand Theft Auto: San Andreas* then questions might be raised about material holdings between specific characters for the purpose of identifying who is impoverished with respect to whom.

Relative poverty is also associated with two related notions: primary poverty and secondary poverty, and both of these terms hold promise for the investigation at hand. Primary poverty is defined as "a situation where income is insufficient to meet basic needs – even if every penny is spent wisely"—and secondary poverty is defined as "a situation where money is misspent on luxuries – leaving insufficient disposal income to buy necessities."[7] Primary and secondary poverty are two valuable concepts for moving toward an analysis of poverty as it is represented in videogames because neither concept necessarily requires a macroeconomic view of a gameplay system. Rather, the analysis can begin with the player's own acts of play and the extent to which they carry the player toward or away from the representations of primary or secondary poverty.

Let's consider how the terms could expand upon or otherwise specify some of the comments on poverty we have encountered so far. If we take Murray's *Casablanca* simulator as a starting point, it enables us to address some of the overlapping frames of mind that Murray assumes would be relevant to play. As those familiar with the film will know, the various stakes of mind Murray identifies—inebriation, infatuation, desire for economic security, and awareness of physical vulnerability—can all be related to the central tension of the film. Hypothetically—and all comments here must be hypothetical, as the game does not exist—the game might have some focus on the concept of secondary poverty—that is, if Rick mis-spends his finances on all the wrong things (i.e., things that do not aid the fight to resist fascist intrusions), then he will indeed be poor. Indeed, should he fail in his resistance, then it might also be concluded that he would fall into a state of primary poverty—as there could be no succeeding economically should the fascist threat gain its troubling goals.

Similar comments might be applied to the other imaginary titles addressed so far, Castronova's *El Dorado* and *World of Poverty*. The "fun economy" Castronova describes for *El Dorado* is essentially a bulwark against the player's perception of—or rumination over—the relevance of poverty to play: absolute poverty does not exist, at least not for the player—as the player is prevented by design from moving into a position where they lack the means to advance.[8] Relative poverty is a distinct possibility for play, to the extent that it serves to compel the player's engagement with deliberate opportunities to advance and develop in the "fun economy." And primary poverty would assumedly be an impossibility in *El Dorado*—but perhaps a possibility in the "less fun" *World of Poverty*. However, the experience of secondary poverty may indeed be part of *El Dorado*, but the consequence of secondary poverty would not be—the player may misspend and fail to meet his or her immediate goals, but the possibility of future movement toward the same or similar goals would assumedly be built into the game.

The terms become much more meaningful when they are applied to commentaries on actual games, such as *State of Emergency* (*SoE*) as addressed by Alexander Galloway and *Second Life* as addressed by Nick Dyer-Witheford and Grieg de Peuter. Galloway comments on *SoE* as follows:

> *State of Emergency*, … the riot game from *Rockstar Games*, has some of these protorealist qualities. The game co-opts the spirit of violent social upheaval, seen in events like the Rodney King rebellion in Los Angeles, California and transposes it into a participatory gaming environment. The game is rife with absurdities and excesses and in no way accurately depicts the brutal realities of urban violence. So in that sense it fails miserably at realism something like a *NARC* for the new millennium. But it also retains a realist core. While the game is more or less realistically rendered, its connection to realism is seen primarily in the representation of marginalized communities (disenfranchised youth, hackers, ethnic minorities and so on), but also in the narrative

> itself, a fantasy of unbridled, orgiastic anti-corporate rebellion. The game slices easily through the apathy found in much mass media today, instructing players to "smash the corporation" and then giving them the weapons to do so.[9]

The central tension in the title—"the fantasy of unbridled, orgiastic anti-corporate rebellion"—can be contextualized as the experience of relative poverty. The "marginalized communities" in *SoE* are endeavoring to "smash the corporation" because of their constrained and deteriorating circumstances. That is to say, they live in a state of relative poverty where it is or has become impossible to spend in ways that maintain an acceptable level of economic stability. At the same time, the corporation that is being smashed can be isolated as the force that has created the conditions of relative poverty, against which these communities are rebelling. In terms of Galloway's larger argument, these defined terms for poverty could enable the critic to bridge the socioeconomic gap between the player and the game. These terms would enable him or her to not only create a precise way to discuss the game, but they would also allow him or her to speak of a hypothetical player's own socioeconomic position with the same term—an assumedly desirable possibility, given that the concept of congruence is central to Galloway's argument.

The ability to specify the player in his or her act of play is also a possibility under the commentary on *Second Life* in *Games of Empire*. In terms of the in-game experience, Dyer-Witheford and de Peuter contend that the infusion of actual dollars into the game creates income disparities between players that enable a 20 percent minority to enjoy fantastic riches while "the rest languish in virtual poverty."[10] Specified conceptions of poverty would enable the authors to be a bit more precise with respect to how these communities are distinguished in the game. For example, how does the concept of fantastic riches relate to the materialist notions associated with absolute or relative poverty? Would "languishing" occur when players are unable to achieve the basic in-game materials that facilitate play for the top 20 percent? Or is it the case that the divide is better specified with the concept of relative poverty—would players be "languishing" only if their holdings—enjoyable or otherwise—were simply fewer in number than those that were possessed by the game's "richest" players? And just how does the divide drive players into primary or secondary poverty?

Just as the terms could be used to specify the experience of play, they could also be used to rescue players of *Second Life* from broad brush generalizations. As already noted, the authors contend that "Playing *Second Life* requires a computer and a broadband connection, which in itself limits access to the upper percentiles of global wealth."[11] The observation bears on the concept of relative poverty, under the notion that access to computers and broadband connections represent material resources that—while not necessary to sustain life—only become available for populations who have a certain percentage of holdings that are greater than those of a minority population. But what does it mean to play *Second Life* from a position of near-relative poverty, or indeed from the position of relative poverty in a community that provides temporary access to such technologies? These questions might be asked, and they might have implications for how players play the game—that is, while "the inhabitants of *Second Life*" might be described as "class-divided, property-owning, commodity-exchanging, currency-trading, networking energy-consuming subjects of a comprehensively capitalist order"[12] what it means for a player to enact such an order from a position proximate to that of relative poverty—secondary or primary—would have meaning for their act of play. The terms promise interpretive possibilities with relevance to established scholarship. The specified conceptions of poverty explored so far provide one avenue for noting how the oppressive and repressive forces of poverty are represented in games and also create one possible framework for associating the player's own economic positioning inside and outside of the game. However, neither the terms nor the critical tradition at hand suggests a definite path for how a detailed investigation into these matters might begin or how it might unfold.

If, then, we continue on with our consideration of videogames as slum simulations—or, more accurately, as slumming simulations—we might now consider the value of these concerns in an extended, contextualizing analysis of a specific title. For example, "relative poverty" and its associated concepts have special significance for our larger consideration of slumming, as they too hinge on distinctions between the evident standards of living in a given societal context—the standards for the slum dweller and the standards for the slumming tourist. A great deal of scholarship concerned with social contexts for gaming has emerged around the title *World of Warcraft*. Generally, this work does not attend to the specific versions or variations of the game that are under direct consideration. This is not necessarily a shortcoming of the critical literature, as there are meaningful gameplay experiences that generally translate between the various updates and gameplay variations, and to the extent that the literature at large is attentive to such matters, it can usually be reconciled with a shared understanding of "the game" writ large. However, it is also the case that the updates, variations, and individual expansions are, of course, all meaningful subjects that contribute to players' shared understanding of the game and its historical development. A similar comment could have been offered with respect to *The Elder Scrolls V: Skyrim* in the previous chapter. In the comments that follow, I will generally only address aspects of play and conceptions of poverty that can be associated with play across a majority of *World of Warcraft*'s various iterations or with versions of the game that have had a significant impact on its overall development.

Academic interest in Blizzard Entertainment emerged in the mid-2000s. While the period was one in which the company received significant attention in the popular press, the academic community paid little attention to either the company or its projects through 2004. Early efforts to associate Blizzard Entertainment with scholarship on videogames are offered by Eric Hayot and Edward Wesp, who offer an observation in passing on the significance of *StarCraft* to Espen Arsenth's theory of ergodic literature.[13] Elsewhere, Sonia K. Katyal offers general comments that reflect awareness of Blizzard Entertainment as part of an argument on the significance of cyberspace to surveillance operations.[14] In both of these examples, the relevance of Blizzard Entertainment is hard to understate, but these works do indicate an essential awareness of the corporation within the academy.

Blizzard Entertainment's essentially invisible presence in the scholarship on videogames through 2004 can be partially attributed to the nascent status of game studies during the first decade of the new millennium and the focus of the field's earliest entries. For example, Janet H. Murray's *Hamlet on the Holodeck: The Future of Narrative in Cyberspace* appeared in 1997, but it would take a number of years before that text would go on to be cited with some frequency in monograph-length works concerned with games, gamers, and gaming: for example, in Edward Castronova's *Synthetic Worlds: The Business and Culture of Online Gaming* (2005), Jesper Juul's *Half-Real: Real Rules and Fictional Worlds* (2006), and Ian Bogost's *Persuasive Games: The Expressive Power of Videogames* (2007). While it would be needlessly reductive—and simply inaccurate—to summarize the pre-2004 literature with a short list of critical intents, the work simply does not lend itself to the kinds of corporate analyses or game-specific commentaries that would become a more regular within the literature in the years following 2004.

Arguably, an important development in the literature that made such criticism possible was the recognition of the significance of economic systems in videogames to everyday life, and of the potential for these systems to become increasingly integrated with everyday life. This notion is expressed with some clarity in Castronova's *Synthetic Worlds*, and it arrives with a number of references to *World of Warcraft* (*WoW*). In the context of Castronova's argument, *WoW* is largely regarded for its potential. That is, Castronova attends to its sales figures and evidence complexity and notes that the game "appears well on the way to becoming the most successful US synthetic world ever."[15]

In the years that followed, *WoW* and Blizzard Entertainment were drawn into a range of academic enterprises with relevance to a broad range of social sciences: psychology, sociology, anthropology, and the humanities—particularly English. It would be an overstatement to say that *Synthetic Worlds* has a direct impact on many of these publications, though several articles did emerge during this time that continued to engage with Castronova's 2005 observations. This is the same period where general interest begins to emerge around titles like *StarCraft* and *Diablo*. However, critical attention during this period is nowhere near as significant as it is for *WoW*, with only a handful of articles emerging on these games through 2010. This basic pattern has persisted to and through the moment of this writing, which can be characterized as one in which hundreds of articles attentive to *WoW* have emerged from academic sources, while the total number of sources attentive to *StarCraft* and *Diablo* is essentially only a couple of dozen. Of course, it would be a mistake to confuse quantity with quality. However, the larger point for the moment is simply to indicate that Blizzard Entertainment's consideration within the academy can be located on or around the middle of the 2000s and that the trajectory of that criticism has been particular attention to *World of Warcraft*. This body of work has relevance to what is currently a novel but potentially productive conversation around poverty within game studies.

Relative Poverty in *World of Warcraft*

Announced in 2001 and launched in 2004, *World of Warcraft* has attracted millions of players and earned billions of dollars since its release. Set primarily in the fantasy realm of Azeroth, the game invites players to undertake thousands of possible quests with avatars drawn from a broad range of fantasy races and occupations. Many of these fantasy races move out into the game world from distinct social systems: humans, elves, dwarves, gnomes, and others are part of the Alliance, while Orcs, Goblins, and the Tauren are aligned with the Horde. While the Alliance and Horde compose distinct social systems, it is also true that each race associated with either faction has its own social context, as do the members of The Burning Legion, and also the simply unaffiliated races in the game.

For the work at hand, I will be tracing the game's poverty theme as it relates to the human race, starting with the character creation and the initial human-related garrison settlement in Northshire. The notion of relative poverty is communicated to players early on in the game, in the character creation process. When they first select their possible class, the player is confronted with what they will later learn is a potential late-stage build for that class. The build appears with formidable weapons and armor that vanish and are replaced by far less impressive undergarments and other soft goods. The transition suggests a diminution with respect not only to material goods but also to capacity. It is in this context that the player is moved into the game's opening narration, which involves a quick movement away from the massive human city of Stormwind and into the remote and less-imposing garrison in Northshire. This physical movement from opulence into the comparatively rural and austere garrison parallels the player's shift from imposing war machine to well-clad farmhand that occurs during character creation. Together, these movements establish an early sense of social contexts for play and of the player's positioning with respect to those contexts—that is, the player is made aware of possible standards for living and is made aware that in their current situations they are existing in a diminished position with respect to those standards.

This notion is immediately affirmed and also complicated by the player's likely first interaction in the game, which is with Marshal McBride. It is true that the player is free to not interact with this individual upon entering the game, but the game positions the player at McBride's feet in such a way that the interaction is probable. McBride indicates that the player is in fact from Stormwind, where the player presumably lived in a diminished economic state prior to the beginning of play, and then offers the player a chance to improve his or her economic position by taking up arms against some invading Blackrock Worgs—wolf-like creatures. For the service, the player is promised Worg handler gloves, a certain amount of experience points, and a certain number of coins. In their immediate context, the rewards suggest the player's movement away from a state of relative poverty into a state of somewhat less dramatic relative poverty. While the essential purpose of the movement is quite abstract, a path has been laid down for the player to follow or not follow, and this gesture is an early manifestation of the game's economic systems and their broad significance to the concept of poverty.

However, the exchange itself is perhaps not as simple as has been described so far. The player does not simply appear at the garrison, but instead is likely to arrive in his or her act of play at a time when there are many other players moving into and out of the same space, characters who are not just arriving, but who are instead actively questing in the area. These players are generally visible to the player as he or she speaks with McBride. They are easily differentiated on the basis of race and class and also, more importantly, on the bases of their clothing armor and weapons, which are likely to be distinct from those of the player who has just arrived in this space. These differences are an early indication of the economic systems and social standards associated with survival in the garrison community. While the reasons, purposes, or costs of these evident differences in material goods are not readily apparent, these goods nevertheless contribute to the player's sense that elevated economic positions are possible. This fact is reinforced in a much more direct way by the garrison's shops, two of which are located near the player when he or she emerges into the play space. Like McBride's questing opportunity, the shops lay out the conditions that need to be met for the player to acquire material items.

Taken together, the game's character creation, opening narration, and early questing opportunities convey the notion that the player is in a diminished state and that she or he has the capacity to move on from that diminished state through action. However, a different commentary on poverty emerges if the game's non-playable characters are considered. For example, consider Marshal McBride. In terms of his evident arms, he appears in an elevated position with respect to the player and also with respect to a number of other characters in the garrison. He is fixed in that position and only stands in the capacity to distribute the promised quest rewards to the player after the player completes a number of tasks in and for the garrison. In this way, McBride and a number of quest-giving non-player characters (NPCs) establish a sense of social stability: they neither rise nor fall in social status and are perpetually in a position to distribute wealth to the player. They do not engage in the kind of tasks that the player engages in, and they acquire only to the extent that their quests are fulfilled. Their economic movement is distinct from the players' characters, and one facet of that difference is their removal from the system of material acquisition outside of the questing structure.

A third layer to this system can be located in the other players who move around the player, who may exchange certain classed and level-capped goods with the player, as well as money. This third level of play may have the effect of assisting the player in his or her movement through the questing structure, but it is essentially distinct from the questing structure, in the sense that it has no bearing on the quests or the quest givers. It reveals the various standards for survival that are available to the player at any given point in the game. All three of these levels convey distinct notions about poverty: the player exists in a diminished state with the possibility for advancement, the quest givers live in a steady state, and the other player characters offer possibilities for exchange and gift giving with relevance to the player's inventory and general holdings.

The fourth aspect of this relationship is the monsters the player interacts with in the course of questing. From these interactions, the player acquires items, coins, and experience, the essential rewards that are generally promised by the quest givers. In this system, the other players cannot give experience to the player, but they can give them the means to acquire more experience, in the sense that they can give them arms, armor, and finances to ease their movement from one quest to the next.

While variations to these basic rules may emerge over the course of play, this essential system is relevant to extended portions of the player's acts of play. It moves with the player and shifts with the player as they journey from one location to the next in the game, but these features are essentially set as the rules of the game that is played by the player in his or her acts of play. What does this tell us about the representation of poverty in *World of Warcraft*? In the game, an essential pathway for the player to engage with any given number of societal contexts is to pursue a quest. In that context, the player is "poor" if they are playing without the resources that are required or that otherwise enable the player to complete the quest and, by that, contribute to the quest's associated social systems.

Because the quests in *World of Warcraft* are essentially tiered, the player's path out of poverty is generally possible, by either completing alternative quests, engaging with their peers, or "grinding" until they have enough resources to succeed in their chosen quest. These activities offer distinct opportunities for play (and various qualitative experiences for play). One of the more interesting features of this system is the persistence with which it works to continually recharacterize the player as existing in a state of relative poverty with respect to each additional quest. That is to say, while certain acquisitions enable the player to exist with relative ease in the context of a given set of quests or other game-related experiences, the player is constantly moving into social contexts that reinforce the notion that, at present, they exist below the necessary standards for advancement. A chief characteristic of the poverty theme in *World of Warcraft*, then, is the unending return to the notion of economic precarity with respect to the unfolding economic systems that determine daily life in Azeroth and beyond.

The relevance of this facet of *WoW*'s poverty theme to the theoretical consideration of videogames considered so far can be expressed as follows. With respect to Murray's comments on the "teetering on the border between a powerfully present illusion and a more authentic but flickering visible ordinary world," the continual reminder of relative poverty can be associated with the player's disequilibrium within "the powerfully present illusion." The flickering of the poverty theme as part of the player's act of play anchors the player to the economic systems of the "ordinary world," even as they estrange the player from that world by virtue of their fantastical elements. In terms of Galloway, the poverty theme would be considered for its association with notions of congruence—that is, with the extent to which the continual communication of relative economic disparity is relative to the player in his or her acts of play. Importantly, this association would require a framework for addressing the player that exceeds the poverty theme itself. For this reason, one clear boundary of this poverty theme for analysis is the economic positioning of the player.

With respect to Castronova, the poverty theme can be considered for its impact on the player's decisions to spend time and money outside of the game space—that is, how effective is the poverty theme in binding the player ever closer in the economic systems of the game and also in deterring them from expanding their economic impact outside of the game space. One answer to this question can be found by considering the poverty theme and its relevance of Dyer-Witheford and de Peuter: to the extent that the poverty theme is already emblematic of the neoliberal conditions of late capitalism, it simply rehearses with might be, under their system, an assumed high level of congruence with the player's act of play. These assumptions find some clarification in the work of Kocurek and Newman, which encourages us to consider the theme in a broader context, both in the context of Blizzard's history as a corporation and in the context of the developing videogame industry.

Contextualizing *World of Warcraft*'s Poverty Themes

In 1991, Allen Adham, Frank Pearce, and Mike Morhaime founded Silicon and Synapse and developed *Radical Psycho Machine Racing*, a game for the Super Nintendo Entertainment System.[16] The title was published by Interplay Productions. *Radical Psycho Machine Racing* (or *RPM Racing*) was a remake of an earlier title for the Commodore 64, *Racing Destruction Set*. Like *Racing Destruction Set*, *RPM Racing* allows players some choice in the design and implementation of their own racetracks. The game proved successful with players and was followed up by a sequel, *Rock N' Roll Racing* in 1993. One of the key distinctions between *Rock N' Roll Racing* and its predecessor, *RPM Racing* (as well as *Racing Destruction Set*), was the removal of the course-generating options that were key elements of those games. In *Rock N' Roll Racing*, players instead encounter a limited role-playing or personalization system that allows for the upgrading of both superficial and performance-specific features for their automobiles. The upgrading system involves the performance-based earnings players receive at the end of each race, which can be spent on upgradable features such as traditional car components—engines, tires, and so on—as well as components related to the game's fanciful opportunities for combat—missiles, mins, and "slip sauce."

Silicon and Synapse released another major title in 1993, *The Lost Vikings* for the Super Nintendo System. It is a side-scrolling adventure title, in which players swap between three Vikings, each with a distinct ability: Erik can run faster than the other Vikings, Baelog can use his bow and arrows to kill enemies from a distance, and Olaf can use his shield to block enemies and their projectiles. Players advance from level to level by selecting between each of these Vikings to navigate a series of challenges. This title also proved successful with players and was followed up by a sequel in 1997.

By 1997, Silicon and Synapse had changed its name twice, first to Chaos Studios in 1993 and then, after the company's acquisition by Davidson and Associates in 1994, to the new much more recognizable Blizzard Entertainment. The first title the company released under that moniker was *Warcraft: Orcs & Humans* in 1994. Much as *RPM Racing* takes its cue from the earlier *Racing Destruction Set*, *Warcraft: Orcs & Humans* is conceptually indebted to earlier works like Technosoft's *Herzog Zwei* (1989) and Westwood Studios' *Dune II* in 1992. *Herzog Zwei* features an economic system that allows the player to acquire mechanized units for combat, and those units must be carefully maintained and often repaired at an expense in the course of play. *Dune II* expanded upon this system with in-game resource gathering opportunities that enabled the player to determine to some degree how quickly they would acquire resources for their developing armies. This system is central to *Warcraft: Orcs & Humans*, as well as to the game's two direct sequels: *Warcraft II: Tides of Darkness* (1995) and *Warcraft III* (2002) and their expansion packs, as well as to Blizzard Entertainment's other major Real-Time Strategy series, *StarCraft* (1998) and *StarCraft II* in 2010.

While *Rock N' Roll Racing* and *Warcraft: Orcs & Humans* present the players with distinct economic systems, these systems are united by related commentaries on economic development. *Rock N' Roll Racing* moves the player to and through a number of reward and exchange opportunities with significance to the player's contexts for play—that is, to the extent that the player chooses to upgrade their vehicles engine or weapons system, they are moving away from player experiences that did not involve such upgrades and into experiences for play that do involve such upgrades. A similar notion can be expressed for *Warcraft: Orcs & Humans*—economic development over time leads to a reordering of player experience from one economically bounded condition to another. While the mechanics and operational logics for these economic systems are distinctive in many ways, these systems can both be located in this general commonality.

The experience of moving from one bounded condition to another manifests in a different way in Silicon and Synapses' *The Lost Vikings*. In this game, the player's opportunities for play are delimited by their chosen Viking's defining skill or skill set. These sets are persistent and essentially unchanging in terms of their distinctiveness with respect to the skill sets of the other Vikings. However, because the player is essentially free to move between these Vikings and their set states, here too gameplay can be understood as touching on an economic system where development—in this case variation—over time leads to a reordering of player experience from one bounded condition to the next. This persistent feature can be associated with another early success for Blizzard, *Diablo* (1996).

Diablo's roots extend to *Moria* (1983), a title inspired by J.R.R. Tolkien's *Lord of the Rings* series, which begins with the player selecting one of a series of bounded states—that is, a race (e.g., human, halfling, or half-elf) and also a class (e.g., Warrior, Mage, or Priest). With respect to *The Lost Vikings*, each of these states comes with a particular skill set—mages can learn magic; priests can learn spells. Unlike *The Lost Vikings*, but like *RPM Racing*, the game allows players to purchase upgrades to their chosen character. In *Moria*, this occurs in a collection of shops—a general store, an armory, a temple, and so on. The ability to modify the bounded state with commerce in *Moria* is also indicative of economic development over time leading to a reordering of player experience from one economically bounded condition to another. This essential system appears in *Diablo*. Though streamlined in terms of the evident races that can be selected. In *Diablo*, the player moves from the ruined town of Tristram into and through a series of random dungeons that lead to the titular villain below. The game was a success with players and was followed up by sequels, *Diablo II* in 2000 and *Diablo III* in 2012.

The Player's Acts of Play: Relative Poverty and Reordered Experience

In each of these titles, the concept of relative poverty is significant to the reordering of player experience. An initial understanding of this relevance and its analytical boundaries can be approached with considerations of the player's act of play in a number of titles we have explored so far. *Rock N' Roll Racing*'s opening sequencing would suggest that some moments are perhaps riper for analysis than others. For example, the game's title screen contains three fairly distinctive humanoid shapes posed in a tableau. These entities present postures commonly associated with heavy metal band posters, a notion that is reinforced by the game's score. Whether these creatures form a society is a good question, and the answer to that question may not be apparent when the crew is removed from view and replaced with a title screen that asks players to select one or two players for the game. This screen anticipates a society of two possible players, rather than suggesting the society the players (one or two) will encounter in the game itself. Another instance asks the player to select their identity in terms of how challenging the course will be "Dookie," "Veteran," or "Warrior."

These instances generate questions about society—some more detailed than others, but they are open to the concept. As the player move into the game, questions about the standards of living associated with particular societies become increasingly evident: first when the player is asked to purchase a vehicle and then in terms of the race conditions themselves, which are designed to imperial the player or players as they move about the course. The parts of the game work together to communicate the society's standards for living, and that conversation begins with the character and machine selection process and then plays out in the racing portions of play. The grammar of character creation leading to imperiled survival can be associated with a number of titles explored so far. For example, it is literally the ongoing condition of *The Lost Vikings*, the society of Vikings is established, and then the player moves between the three Vikings to overcome the threats to survival that block the society from persisting in its goals. *Moria* and *Diablo* also establish a basic society in their opening moments, to the extent that character creation indicates the kinds that can be or are associated with the player's possible acts of play. The same can be said of *Warcraft: Orcs & Humans.* That game begins with a general overview of the social tensions between Humans and Orcs, and then it invites the player to select either humans or orcs to begin their journey into the world. This essential feature of play can be found in the *Warcraft* sequels. *StarCraft* begins with a similar introduction to the basic social tensions that are relevant to the game and its world. However, it does not allow the player to select their starting point. They must play as Terran (human) and move through the subsequent adventures to gain access to the other lifeforms in the game.

While distinct, notions of society and threats to survival are essentially communicated in all of these titles. However, the games start to differentiate from one another when the notion of given societal context is taken into consideration. For example, *Rock N' Roll Racing* takes place across a possible total of six planets, all of which have their own themes and dangers for the player. In terms of setting, *Rock N' Roll Racing* provides the six themed worlds, which are defined by their frightful racetracks—an entirely hostile landscape for the racing culture that moves to and through each landscape's various tracks. The prevailing standards for living in each of these similar social contexts are related to the player's vehicular capacities, the capacities the player brings to the game both in terms of their vehicle navigation and in terms of the various attributes the player associates with these vehicles through purchase agreements in the game's various shopping instances. To be impoverished in such a world is to fall below the prevailing standards for any given track. Poverty here, then, is associated with the act of losing, but it is not defined by the act of losing. That is, the player can survive a race and still lose the race. Instead, death and losing are tied together as possible states of impoverishment in the game.

This essential notion of social context can be translated to *The Lost Vikings*. Like *Rock N' Roll Racing*, *The Lost Vikings* contains a number of themed settings, within which there are various levels the player moves through on his or her way to the end of the title. There are thirty-seven such levels in all, and within each of these worlds, the setting surrounding the player is hostile to the player's movement. The prevailing standards for living in all of these environments can be largely defined by the special capacities of the Vikings—that is, in order to survive the Vikings must bring their general as well as their special abilities to bear on the landscape and its hostile elements. Failing to do so, the player falls below the prevailing standards for survival, a status that involves either a failure to advance through the gamespace—much as the player who fails to navigate into a winning position in *Rock N' Roll Racing* fails to advance onward to the next track and/or planet—or "dying" in the game and losing one of a limited number of lives.

Diablo's social context follows a similar trajectory. The player's movement through four themed environments involves passage to and through sixteen total levels. While the dungeons in *Diablo* are famously random in terms of their construction, their social context is essentially the same as the contexts found in *Rock N' Roll Racing* and *The Lost Vikings*. That is to say, in their various formats, the settings all establish a hostile track where the prevailing standards for living are related to the player's capacities to navigate the track and, as part of that navigation, deploy their character's various attributes for survival, some of which are germane to the player's chosen class and some of which are common to all play possibilities in the game. To fall below the standards for survival in any given portion of the game is to fail to advance and, frequently, to die. Relative poverty in all three games has essentially similar implications for the player's act of play—it is to be arrested and, frequently, to perish.

Similar claims can be made about the role of relative poverty in *Warcraft: Orcs & Humans*, *Warcraft II*, and *Warcraft III*, as well as for *StarCraft* and *StarCraft II*. Each game moves the player through campaigns or acts that are divided into segmented experiences. Movement to and through each of these experiences involves the player's successful navigation with resources with a series of hostile environments. Failure to achieve or meet the prevailing standards of living in all of these environments comes with the likely consequence of failing to move on from an immediate environment and destruction. Across these titles, then relative poverty has common features and implications: it is associated with geographic isolation and destruction. While each of these games has its own unique methods for representing these features of poverty, the features themselves are common to all of the titles.

World of Warcraft Poverty Thematics

Poverty as such undergoes an interesting development in Blizzard's *World of Warcraft* series (2004–). Just as *RPM Racing* and *Diablo* can trace their roots to earlier titles, *World of Warcraft* owes a great deal to games such as *Neverwinter Nights* (1991) and *EverQuest* (1999). *Neverwinter Nights* popularized the notion of multiple players being ranked against one another in an online environment, and, over the course of the 1990s, expanded in its opportunities for online player interaction. *EverQuest* iterated on the kinds of player interactions that were available in *Neverwinter Night* by radically expanding opportunities for player interaction—role-playing, combat, and simple persistence with other players in a shared environment. In terms of social context, these and related titles indicate new pathways for considering in-game settings and cultural interactions. On one hand, a consideration of social contexts in *Neverwinter Nights* and *EverQuest* can overlap with considerations of social contexts in *Rock N' Roll Racing*, *The Lost Vikings*, or *Diablo*. Each game has its own distinct regions, which have their own perils for the player with challenges to navigation and expenditure. Similarly, in *Neverwinter Night* and *EverQuest*, a player's failure at navigation will result in geological isolation and/or destruction. However, in these titles the consequences of geological isolation are distinct from those found in the early Blizzard titles explored so far. As a participant in a shared and persistent gamespace, the player is surrounded by a world that is shaped by other players' movements to and through their shared geography. That is to say, the evident values for a given region's standards for living are routinely demonstrated and affirmed in ways that do not necessarily bear on the player's own progression through the shared space. This aspect of play is transformative for the concept of relative poverty. The economic status of other members of society, at least as that status can be associated with notions of survival within discrete contexts, becomes significant to the player's act of play—not only in the sense that other players can become targets or sources of assistance but also in the sense that the representation of other players is also often a representation of the manifold economic pathways to success (or destruction) in the world. That is to say, other players become evidence of the game's expansive and extremely nuanced "standards for living" at any given moment in the game.

As the possible standards for living expand, what it means for a player to fall below those standards also changes. This is because the players that might surround the player at any given moment of play are not necessarily players who simply meet the standards for living in a given environment. Rather, the game's relatively open-ended structure means that players might be significantly overprepared to survive in a given environment. A player in a region they might overwise dominate with their meager holdings might fall victim to a player with outsized access to means that are far beyond those of the player with otherwise appropriate goods and capacities. In short, the persistent nature of this shared world destabilizes notions of how and when and under what conditions a player can be assured that they have met the social standards for survival in a given region.

But there is another aspect to such play that pertains not so much to the standards for living but to broader questions of setting itself: that is, what does the character bring to his or her settings as she or he moves through the world? In early titles like *Neverwinter Nights*, what the player brings is their recorded score, which is left as an indicator of both possibility and success within a given instance, much in the way a score would be left on an arcade machine in an earlier era. That score suggests a certain history of play, even if the history is only indicated through the abstraction of acquired and recorded points. However, in a game like *EverQuest*, that history has a partial, explicit representation in the player's evident stats and as well as their material holdings—the weapons, armor, and spells that they carry with them from one region to the next and in the process become a spectacle for other players.

The network of such appearances in a given location constitutes an evident standard of living with respect to the challenges to persistence that are also associated with the same location. This is an economic reality that can be associated with, but which is also distinct from, the evident opportunities for financial exchange or reward in the same location. Such opportunities are essentially static unless they are modified by player or population involvement. They are also bound in ways that the flowing population is not bound. This layer of play changes the relative simplicity of the geographic boundaries for relative poverty to the extent that it expands radically the possibilities for action in the location that are possible from any number of characters that may be significantly more developed than the player's character. This expansion also undermines the player's ability to conceptualize social context with the ease the player may experience in, say, *Rock N' Roll Racing* or *The Lost Vikings*. The evident spectrum of possibility is realized in passing, as it is as fleeting as the movement of other characters to and through the shared space.

In this context, the player's effort to develop on any number of fronts—in experience, in holdings, in reputation—is an effort to move with respect to the evident standard of living. As the player is generally free to move about a number of regions in the game, he or she does this with some limited agency to modify his or her immediate standards of living, as they may move to a region that is more or less hostile to survival, given the status of the player's character at any given moment. In this system, the notion of relative poverty is substantially distinct from the notions considered in titles like *Rock N' Roll Racing*, *The Lost Vikings*, and *Warcraft: Orcs & Humans*. Relative poverty is not tied so tightly to notions of geographic status and death. *World of Warcraft* allows the player the consequence or relative poverty or the pursuit. That is to say, in this game the player is literally allowed to be poor with very few immediate consequences. Consequences certainly do appear should the player wander into a confrontation well beyond their capacities and holdings. In general, though, through no fault of their own or by deliberate choice, the player can *be poor and remain poor* in the context of an environment.

The player's ability to choose poverty can be distinguished from representations of poverty that he or she may encounter in the course of play itself. For example, just as the evident holdings and capacities of the social environment suggest standards of living within a given region, many regions in *World of Warcraft* include non-playable characters and dwellings that further qualify the meaning of relative poverty within a given location. To continue with the garrison at the beginning of the game, the player's movement to and through this portion of the game put them into contact with what appears to be a privative economic system: in the context of the military outpost there are private merchants, farmers, and other characters who harvest the surrounding forest. While there is some diversity in this group of non-player characters, with respect to the standards of living represented by the players, these individuals present as incapable of engaging in combat with the wargs, orcs, kobolds, and gnolls that trouble the region.

While these evident divisions are a meaningful part of the player's act of play, it is also the case that the consequences of poverty are extremely particular. For example, in *Rock N' Roll Racing*, poverty is consequential to geographic positioning and survival. In *World of Warcraft*, poverty is also consequential to geographic positioning and survival, but there are manifold possibilities for persisting in a state of relative poverty that are not afforded to players of *Rock N' Roll Racing*. To fall into poverty in *Rock N' Roll Racing* is to risk the immediacy of loss, but that is not the case in *World of Warcraft*. One can be poor and simply persistent as poor until one presses onward into conditions that exceed one's capacities. The notion of persistence then is a key feature of the game's poverty theme. However, while persistence in poverty is a distinguishing characteristic of the game, it is also true that *World of Warcraft* is by design organized to encourage the player into broad and broadening experiences that increase wealth and status within the game. This forward momentum works contrary to the possibility of persistence that itself works to further enmesh the player in increasingly specific and detailed economic categories. This pressure to acquire and adapt over time often turns the possibility of persistence into an absurdity—that is, one should not "waste one's time" in the game in that way, as there are so many evident things to be done or accomplished that bring added value to the game experience that are not accessible if one simply "persists."

But even as the game discourages the player from simply persisting in a given state, it is also the case that the player's ability to do exactly that is necessary for economic development over time to be a meaningful concept in the game: one does not desire to persist because persistence delays the satisfaction of acquiring. The game's so-called grinding dynamic speaks to this tension. Players lacking sufficient means are relegated to prowling again and again through the same territories, looking for a number of enemies they can surely best in order to, at a painfully slow rate, move toward their next major increase in level, holdings, or status. These kinds of experiences underscore the notion that relative poverty is to be avoided, to the extent that it literally traps the player in a loop of uninteresting, repeated actions that only very slowly deliver them to the next development in play. To the extent that players are willing to engage in such behavior, they demonstrate a willingness to tolerate persistence in poverty under the promise of eventual economic liberation. While grinding shows the intersection of relative poverty and economic aspiration in *World of Warcraft*, this intersection should not be confused with notions of simple persistence, which occur beyond the bounds of grinding. Rather, it is through the player's non-productive existence, or in their simple wandering without economic distinction, that they persist.

Persistence, of course, is not a status that is particular to players in a specific state of relative poverty. However, the nature of the game is such that player's movement is tied to their general level of advancement, and so a higher-level player not only has more in terms of evident holdings than a lower-level player, but they also have more opportunities to persist in a steady state. While it is true that any player at any state can simply log in and do nothing, players with a history of in-game accomplishments can choose to do nothing in a wider variety of spaces and places.

To further understand the poverty theme, these notions need to be considered in more detail. Spatial isolation in *Rock N' Roll Racing* occurs when the player is unable to advance from one racetrack to the next, due to a failure to navigate the track into one of the three top positions. The consequence of the impoverishment is the experience or repetition. This experience can be limited or extended, depending on the severity of the player's impoverishment. This is similar to the consequences of impoverishment in *The Lost Vikings*. There, a failure to attain the social standards for survival has as a consequence the need to replay the scenario that resulted in the player's failed navigation. Here too the reward of poverty is repetition. This is also a central experience in *Diablo*. When the character dies, they not only die but have the added complication of losing their material holdings, which they must journey toward and recapture as part of their experience of re-playing the game to their point of failure. Re-playing to and through an explored space is, then, part of the poverty dynamic in all of these titles when poverty is associated with death.

This essential condition extends to *World of Warcraft*. There, when the player "dies," they are given several options. In a spectral form, they can physically journey to their dropped goods, or they can choose to respawn with consequences for their holdings. This choice equates the experience of spectral wandering—during which the player cannot interact with other members of the world—with the consequences of material loss. The player's ability to choose within certain boundaries is a choice that does not appear in the earlier works considered so far. The spectral wandering extends the experience of geographic isolation with additional constraints: the player is free to move about for a time without encountering damage or threat, but they are reduced to the status of a spectator, bound to watch and do nothing else. The status effectively takes the player out of the social context, though it does have some values for player positioning and strategy and how they evaluate the threat in an environment before they recapture their fallen arms. However, the freedom to choose to respawn and potentially move in a different direction from the direction that brought their recent doom is a possibility that sets the title apart from earlier titles. Certainly, it is totally in keeping with the open world nature of the game.

The implications of death for future play are one of the ways in which the poverty theme has particular relevance to the player's acts of play. In World of Warfract, a third facet of the theme relates to the game's system of promised and random wages. The absurdity of work and reward is baked into the questing structure, to the extent that material goods, currency, and experience points are organized and promised as reimbursement for the player's focused acts of play. The questing structure indicates a path toward progress, and while the rewards for that progress may at times appear to make a certain amount of sense, at other times the rationale for reimbursement is quite mysterious. In this system, the player can generally choose to quest for specific rewards or quest for random acquisitions (or, of course, choose to do neither). However, when these choices are made, they establish a contract of sorts between the player's act of play and the social context in the game. While the reward system is not necessarily less absurd in *Rock N' Roll Racing* or *The Lost Vikings*, the player has less choice in terms of his or her decision to participate in the exchange system—the way forward in these titles is limited and sometimes so narrowly imagined that it can only be pursued along a single course, pun intended. *Diablo* shares some similarities with *World of Warcraft*, particularly in a title like *Diablo III*, as the game encourages multiple playthroughs in the pursuit of increasingly strange and abstract items for the player to differentiate his or her characters from other player's characters.

These three aspects of the player's acts of play in *World of Warcraft* constitute a poverty theme. The theme finds its origin in earlier titles, some of which can also be associated with Blizzard Entertainment. The relevance of the theme across these titles is not necessarily a phenomenon unique to the works of Blizzard Entertainment, but it does establish a way to think about or address poverty as it exists with and between these titles.

The value of this way of thinking is that it not only offers a specific understanding of the player's act of play, but it also establishes a common point for the consideration of multiple articles and monographs that touch on related notions.

Beyond the Slums: The Player's Act of Play as Context for Poverty Thematics

To the extent that poverty can be identified as a theme relevant to the player's act of play, it might be considered in terms of its evident, collective gameplay features. This notion moves us inexorably toward a second challenge for the work that follows: namely, how might such features be resolved or otherwise aligned with the player's act of play? This is, how might they facilitate or potentially undermine the act itself? To argue that one game is exceptionally ripe for such analysis is to assert a disingenuous, totalizing knowledge of the field *and* of the player's assumed economic positioning. So, rather than do that, let's agree that the work that follows is only an effort to model such analysis and not to establish a definitive assessment of a poverty theme's relevance to a broad conception of players at play: let us explore what can be done, rather than assert understanding of what cannot (yet) be known.

We can begin to move toward such modeling by considering again our borrowed definition for relative poverty, which defines poverty "in relation to the economic status of other members of the society." This definition suggests that economic comparisons relevant to individual players would be precursors for detailed investigations not only of a poverty theme but of that theme's interpreted relevance to the player's act of play. With respect to relative poverty, one title that can be associated with particular conceptions of relative poverty associated with specific players is Blizzard's *Hearthstone*. A rationale and justification for such associations in my larger argument can be located in the notion that *Hearthstone*'s poverty theme has had a dramatic and documentable impact on the game's global reception in recent years. Arguably, the theme has come to color public perception of the game and is, for some populations, itself a gateway for play.

In the spring of 2018, the Chinese Communist Party expressed a desire for novel legal means to extradite individuals from Hong Kong. This development was met by a series of massive and sustained protests that received near-continuous coverage from news agencies such as the BBC[17] and *New York Times*. Across the continents, demonstrations in support of Hong Kong's furious citizens were held both on and off-line. One such protest occurred in October of that year, at a Blizzard-hosted *Hearthstone* tournament for the Asia-Pacific region. While being interviewed by Taiwanese journalists, professional *Hearthstone* player Chung Ng Wai cried out in Mandarin, "Liberate Hong Kong, revolution of our times!"[18] Chung's interviewers reacted to the demands by literally diving behind a desk. Blizzard Entertainment's reaction to the scene was equally craven: the corporation decided to take away "10,000 in winnings" from Chung and to bar him from playing *Hearthstone* for a year. These actions, later revised, resulted in a public relations disaster: players and politicians alike decried the punishment and heckled Blizzard for its willingness to debase itself to please China.

One of the more interesting—and to the best of my knowledge yet-to-be-explored—facets of the Blizzard/Chung debacle is *Hearthstone*'s own capacity to frame the incident and its associated fallout. *Hearthstone* is an online strategy card game with fantasy themes in the tradition of *Magic: The Gathering*. According to Blizzard, the game is "for everyone" and "easy to learn but hard to put down."[19] Players can choose to engage with the game in a number of distinct modes. With jocular prose, Blizzard explains that players can "practice [their] skills in Casual play, climb the ranks in Ranked mode, shake things up with crazy fun Tavern brawls, test [their] luck in the Arena, play solo adventures against fiendishly clever computer opponents, and much, much more."[20] While *Hearthstone* adapts many of its gameplay features from *Magic: The Gathering*, the game is populated with extensive references to Blizzard's own *World of Warcraft* franchise. Players take on the persona of one of several possible characters from the franchise and then "battle it out" with cards depicting various powers, people, and places associated with the *World of Warcraft*'s games or supplementary products.

By the time of Chung's protest, the original *Hearthstone* game had been expanded to include eight themed card collections that players could integrate into the main game. Four of those sets are associated with narratives depicting an isolated community under direct threat by a destabilizing entity. For example, *Rise of Shadows* is concerned with the *League of Evil*'s efforts to take over the floating city of Daraland. *Saviors of Uldum* is literally about an effort to extradite Daraland to Uldum. *Whispers of the Old Gods* is about Azeroth being corrupted by an outside force, and *The Witchwood* is concerned with the imperiled Kingdom, Gilneas, efforts to band together to fight off an evil encroaching witch, Hagatha, who has corrupted a nearby forest.

It is not surprising that *Hearthstone* would turn to such narratives with some frequency. This game's fantasy elements—wizards, witches, dragons, thieves, elves, and the like—can be associated with what Northrup Frye identifies as "the sentimental romance," an ancient storytelling practice that traces the development of an individual through a series of magical adventures concerned with interacting and intersecting supernatural communities.[21] Key to this tradition is notions of communal contributions that stand in opposition to an existential threat. Blizzard has capitalized on such storytelling for a long time: *The Lost Vikings* illustrates three Vikings sharing their unique abilities to overcome an alien invasion; the *World of Warcraft* titles all concern player development of fantasy outposts that work together to overcome a foe or foes—the same can be said of the *StarCraft* titles; the *Diablo* titles all follow a hero on a journey to confront ultimate evil with the assistance of one or more communal settlements. *Overwatch* draws from this tradition too, with its balanced player groups working cooperatively to overcome an enemy or enemies.

Given the significance of sentimental romance to Blizzard's bottom line, the corporation's reaction to Chung's protest is noteworthy, at least to the extent that it allows for a distinction to be made between select narrative values and business interests. Of course, it is unreasonable to assume that any competitive organization would operate with something like a strict adherence to fairy-tale virtues. Nevertheless, it is fascinating to note that gameplay concerned with such virtues occasioned Chung's protest and that Blizzard found itself a victim of its own narrative practices by failing to recognize the social significance of such values to its player base.

With respect to *Hearthstone*, the player's act of play is associated with a limited number of "mana crystal" points that might be spent in each round of play. In the first round of play, the first player has one point to spend, and the second player has one point also—but also the option to spend a second point with a "coin" card. In the second round of play, the first player has two points to spend, and the second player does too, and so on and so forth until both players have a maxim of ten points to spend in any given turn. These values can be adjusted at various moments by select cards or other gameplay abilities, but gameplay is essentially facilitated by the choices a player makes to spend their points during any given turn. The issue of primary poverty can be associated with the question of whether or not a player in the context of play has sufficient income (points) to meet basic needs. In the context of *Hearthstone*, the concept of basic needs can be conceptualized simply as the capacity to persist to the next round of play. Primary poverty would occur—or be most acute—when no spending decisions open to the player would result in his or her persistence through the next round. Secondary poverty would occur when the player misspends points with the consequences of being left with no point spending options to persist through the next round. The distinction between these two scenarios is a distinction between opportunity and action. In the secondary poverty scenario, the failure to persist could be tied to an evident error in spending. In the primary poverty scenario, the option to spend "correctly" was itself not an option for the player or at least is no longer an option in the game's evident economic systems. With respect to how this can help us understand the game: the progressive income associated with each turn, and the accumulation of turns, suggests that player failure is generally correlated with secondary poverty—that is, failure comes about as misspending leads to a situation where spending can no longer be sustained, under the collective consequences of misspending.

While the game may convey or affirm the threat of secondary poverty as part of play, the issue of primary poverty—and the anxiety around that poverty—can be associated with the individual cards and their association with a player's "deck" in any given game. At this point, these observations of the player's act of play can be associated with another feature of the game, one that reinforces the relevance of primary and secondary poverty to the player's act of play. *Hearthstone* enables the player to acquire new cards in one of two ways: the player can accumulate wins and be rewarded for those wins with a pack of cards, or the player can choose to purchase a pack or packs of cards through an in-game store, with national currencies such as the dollar. With respect to the first option, the reward system is based on notions of player persistence—that is, their in-game choices allow them to sustain the basic necessities of life longer than their opponent is able to. As a "winner" the player creates an opportunity for considering both absolute and relative poverty. Absolute poverty occurs for the losing player, the moment they are unable to maintain basic living/playing standards. The experience of absolute poverty in a game like *Hearthstone* is associated with the climax of play—the status is achieved at the same moment the game terminates. Indeed, the event coincides with the appearance of an image of the player's in-game avatar appearing in rather rough and discombobulated shape, while the winner is treated to an image of their in-game avatar appearing triumphant. However, what happens next is perhaps most telling about the fantasy of absolute poverty that is presented in this title: the losing player is typically rewarded with some minimal amount of experience toward their next level of play—not as much as the winning player, but enough to convey the notion that even in defeat the player is progressing toward increased status and expertise. This is a quality of absolute poverty as it is presented in the game. The key here is the notion that absolute poverty has a small not nevertheless positive implication for the player.

At the conclusion of play, the concept of relative poverty is conveyed in a different way, but with a similar outcome. It is conveyed in the game's player-ranking system, which periodically resets. Players work their way up from a low level to a higher-ranked level through progressive and sustained wins. This provides a basic metric in which lower levels can be associated with less accumulated wins in a given season or ranking period. Under this model, medium status can be associated with mid-tier rankings. However, again, one of the interesting features of play is that the game does not reveal all of its rankings to the player at any given moment. A player may work from twenty-five up to level one and then finds him or herself in a new-higher tier, which itself can be subdivided into numerical or color-coded categories. The system creates various segmented status levels that might convey notions of relative poverty within or between the levels. As a consequence, relative poverty is indeed truly relative, but more important is the notion that the experience of escaping relative poverty always comes with the gut punch that the escape was illusory—there are almost always other hills to climb. The notions of primary and secondary poverty can be associated with this climb: primary poverty occurs when the player simply does not have the card set—however acquired—to keep moving up the tiered roster, and secondary poverty occurs when the player mismanages resources in a way so as to prevent their progression up the roster—that is, they play too poorly to advance.

With respect to the notion of Castronova's fun economy, or the concept of virtual poverty—and even with respect to Galloway's concept of convergence—there is a key observation to be made here: *Hearthstone* offers players intertwined and—importantly—qualified experiences of both absolute and relative poverty. These experiences are offered in such a way as to suggest that both the player and the game are advancing, even when the player falls into state of poverty. The key observation here is that the system depends on the experience of poverty—and not only that—but on the experience of poverty denied. This relates to a related feature of the game: the promise of abundance. The player is always acquiring new points to spend and new cards to play as long as they do not run over the pre-set limits. Spending does have immediate implications for play, but there is always the promise of renewal, as long as one manages to persist into the next round of play. This related feature of play is another way in which the necessary evils of in-game poverty and want are softened for the player.

Poverty is significant to the player's act of play in *Hearthstone*. The title's various and often related forms of in-game currency (coins, wins, experience, rankings) fashion a complicated pattern of falling into or avoiding absolute as well as relative poverty. This experience is informative of the player to the extent that it describes the player's in-game status in the context of the game's larger efforts to represent and deny a poverty experience or experiences of poverty. Indeed, it suggests the player is deliberately engaged with play experiences that are designed to keep at arm's length actual encounters with poverty. Similarly, the presentation of poverty in *Hearthstone* suggests the game is grounded in, and to a large sense determined by, a desire to present such opportunities to the player. Should such a desire be relevant to the game—that is, to its design and the player's acts of play—then is it reasonable to wonder about the impetus for such relevance—can it be located in some subject external to the game?

Notes

1. Ruiz, 136.
2. Krcmar, 89.
3. Sicart, 28.
4. Hill, 83.
5. www.thehumanperspective.co.uk
6. Ibid.
7. Economicshelp.org
8. Castronova, Chapter 8.
9. Galloway, "Social."
10. Dyer-Witheford, *Games*, 104.
11. Ibid., 106.
12. Ibid., 119.
13. Hayot and Wesp. "Style and Mimesis."
14. Katyal, "The New Surveillance."

15. Castronova, 4606.
16. References to the historical development of Blizzard are in reference to claims from *activisionblizzard.com*
17. BBC, https://www.bbc.com/news/world-asia-china-44674982
18. Victor, https://www.nytimes.com/2019/10/09/world/asia/blizzard-hearthstone-hong-kong.html?searchResultPosition=2
19. Playhearthstone.com
20. Ibid.
21. Frye, *Secular.*

Bibliography

Castronova, Edward. *Synthetic Worlds: The Business and Culture of Online Games.* Chicago: University of Chicago Press, 2005. Kindle edition.

EverQuest, Daybreak Game Company, 1999.

StarCraft. Blizzard Entertainment, 1998.

StarCraft II. Blizzard Entertainment, 2010.

Warcraft II: Tides of Darkness. Blizzard Entertainment, 1995.

Warcraft III. Blizzard Entertainment, 2002.

CHAPTER 3

Player Identity and the Conditions of Play

Playing at Poor

The view of thematized poverty dynamics considered so far recognizes an essential tension in play—a desire to risk the experience of poverty counterbalanced by a firm commitment to gameplay dynamics that prevent such experiences from either manifesting or persisting for any significant length of time. While the concept of slumming provides a basic rationale for this tension, that rationale is founded on a particular conception of the player that may or may not be warranted in a given instance of the player's act of play. For example, while slumming's Victorian roots might be traced across the twentieth and now the twenty-first century, these roots do not themselves reveal the particular connective tissues that assumedly express and retain interest in slumming in the contexts of particular games. An exploration of such concerns requires increased attention to the contexts of play itself—that is, the industrial and cultural conditions of gaming that can—or, more importantly, might—be associated with the player's act of play at a given point or points in time.

The history of the industry's oftentimes bumpy road to mainstream appeal has become increasingly relevant to scholarly contributions of the academic area known as game studies. In recent years, noteworthy critics have made the cultural conditions of play itself a fascinating subject of study. Such work has enabled students and scholars alike to envision their lived experiences with gaming both as shaping and as shaped by their

A. Crowley, *Representations of Poverty in Videogames*,
https://doi.org/10.1007/978-3-031-00144-4_3

culture's developmental turns. As noted in Chap. 1, Kocurek and Neuman's texts both offer productive considerations of the videogame industry's significance to middle-class audiences, particularly to boys and young men, and their work reviews the various means and methods that industry and industry-adjacent organizations have deployed to attract and retain audiences across what are now multiple generations. While their work should not be confused with the panicked scolding of moral reformers and the like, much of what is best in game studies today is ironically indebted to our nation's early reactionary voices, in the sense that our scholarship is carrying on and specifying the notion that personal identity is consequential to a player's interactions with videogames.

That tension, addressed with such consideration in Gray and Leonard's *Woke Gaming*, provides added context for the rhetorical tropes that surround and sustain conversations on poverty in that text. That is, to the extent that the editors and the authors are moving into complicated notions of identity, they are engaging with the tangled web of socioeconomic factors that delimit the player's worldview and self-conceptions. In that context, it is quite reasonable that notions like poverty would first emerge in a stacked deck of related social ills: for example, alongside crime, hunger, and general conceptions of violence. This is what it looks like when a discipline moves toward increasingly specific considerations of culture. That movement involves a necessarily broadening of perspective beyond initial considerations of potential forms and functions so that the conditions that both produce and sustain interest in such subjects can be identified and analyzed.

However, at the same time, it is true that such considerations require their own conceptual undergirding, and the works considered so far suggest that identity—understood generally or with some sophistication—is an animating field-specific force that is working to that effect. General conceptions of poverty and its portrayals can be framed with notions of identity: that is, what are the consequences of poverty for the player's acts of play? How might it shape players' in-game experiences and, more broadly, their conceptions of poverty beyond the act of play? While the focus on poverty as such is fairly novel in Gray and Leonard's collection, the essential observation that videogames inspire questions about representation has long-standing relevance to game studies. A foundation for the discipline's attention to this issue can be located in Janet H. Murray (1997). There, Murray considers the then-novel storytelling capacities of late twentieth-century computational technologies and addresses their possible implications for life in the twenty-first century. In the course of her argument, she affirms a conceptual division between so-called virtual or hyperreal subjects and their "real world" counterparts.[1] She asserts that our experiences with such subjects involve a "teetering on the border between a powerfully present illusion and a more authentic but flickering visible ordinary world." The notion that the so-called ordinary world is more authentic than hyperreality's powerful present illusion has analytical implications for represented subjects in videogames.[2] Chief among these implications is the contention that authenticity is itself a productive concept for understanding our interactions with narrative structures that emerge from computational technologies. This notion is highly charged, as notions of authenticity suggest an arbiter of the authentic. Murray does not move to detail this matter, but her lack of specificity does not undermine her essential point, which might be characterized as follows: the player's act of play is rooted in perceptions that precede and exceed the act.

This notion squares nicely with conceptions of slumming addressed in the previous chapters, as the concept of slumming is based on more than just a joyful ogling of the curious poor by affluent adventurers. That is, there is a necessary movement into and out of the slum space, a descent into poverty, and a retreating ascent or return to the slumming individual's elevated residence or home. For all parties involved, such movements come with questions of when, why, and under what conditions the reality of slummed space can be aligned with the space of the fortunate adventure. However that line might be drawn—before, during, or after the poverty safari—the line is riddled with questions bearing on notions of transgression and perception—when and under what conditions is the experience of poverty authentic for the slumming individual, can it even be authentic, and under what conditions might it appear to be more or less authentic. And, more importantly, how do these same conceptions of authenticity relate to the represented community?

Efforts to address the significance of authentic, class-based representations in games to the player's act of play emerged in the early 2000s. Examples of such scholarship include the already addressed works by Alexander Galloway's "Social Realism in Gaming" and Edward Castronova's *Synthetic Worlds: The Business and Culture of Online Games*. With respect to Murray, Galloway and Castronova offer arguments that consider individuals "teetering on the border" between digital, storytelling contexts and broader, social situations. With respect to the focus of this book, Galloway's and Castronova's works are crucial, as they generate an initial-if-limited vocabulary for talking about videogames and classed representations within videogames. For example, Galloway makes the useful observation that the player's acts of play can be described in terms of the player's cultural contexts and notes that videogame designers can be more or less attentive to these contexts with the possibilities for interaction they program into their products.[3] Galloway offers the previously noted term "congruence" to denote gameplay experiences that involve a high level of fidelity between such contexts and the opportunities for action represented in a game. With respect to Murray's argument, congruence can be regarded as a special instance of "teetering," one in which the game's powerfully present illusion is substantiated with opportunities for action that have localized significance for the player in his or her act of play. Galloway's observation is insightful, but it is also narrow in the sense that congruence constitutes a special state of play. For example, any specified understanding of players should carry with it the notion that social contexts are discrete and fluid between communities. A similar observation can be made about game design practices and the need for game designers to construct titles that will be received across vast geographic regions with any number of competing cultural concerns. "Congruence" is a noteworthy concept, but in terms of Galloway's argument, it seems more of a possibility for niche titles than for titles with moderate or broad appeal.

However, and in all fairness to Galloway, it should be noted that he is not overly concerned with the immediate limits of congruence as an analytical term because he is offering the term as a tool to facilitate a larger polemic on how games should engage with their players, and vice versa. As we will see in Chap. 5, game studies has noteworthy scholarly traditions concerned with questions about what videogames should do and also questions about how videogames might be conceptualized. From a contemporary perspective, one in which the market for digital entertainment experiences has grown so vast and complicated, such notions may feel quaint or naïve. However, such feelings are actually, themselves, quite naïve, to the extent they overlook the literal decades of cross-cultural conversations on games, gamers, and gaming that have shaped the conditions of play and also the related conversations on middlebrow entertainments that, as we will see later, have been so central to the development of middle-class communities in the United States across the nineteenth, twentieth, and now twenty-first centuries.

For his part, Castronova works to move such conversations away from entrenched notions of how games should function by considering instead how games do function, at least with respect to economic systems. He offers a consideration of related matters in his comments on "synthetic worlds" or "playgrounds of the imagination" emerging from the computer game industry that, he asserts, have become an "important host of ordinary human affairs."[4] Some of these affairs are economic, and Castronova considers how games can construct "fun economies" that give players "a meaningful role to play," one that can be associated with notions of ownership. He provides a general listing of the basic gameplay qualities that should be included in such economies: for example, property, theft, jail, and major events and epochs at the macro level. In the course of his argument, he turns to the potential consequences that fun economies might have for general industries, such as the terrestrial and space-based tourism industries. He writes, "When Tahiti is only a few clicks away, why take a flight there?" He also asks, "When I already own a [space]ship that can fly me to Alpha Centauri … why support a space program that's just getting to Mars?"[5] Such questions portend what Castronova views as a possible consequence of the game-based hosting of economic systems: "a weakening of support" for related affairs that occur outside of the gameplay with additional "costs and complications." In terms of Galloway's conception of "congruence," Castronova's comments underscore the notion that the opportunities for action a game affords its players can be used to characterize the significance of such opportunities to the player's cultural situation. With respect to Murray, Castronova's comments imply that players do not necessarily "teeter" in their acts of play, at least not as participants in "fun economies." "Teetering" brings to mind chaotic if not random action. Instead, player action in the context of a fun economy might be understood as a guided enacting of inculcated cultural practices associated with capitalism. Castronova's implied awareness of such practices is not offered with a substantiating exploration of how those practices might be enforced in a modern economic system, though it is true that he attends to the subject of economic policy at multiple points in his argument and that his comments on economic policy suggest practical relationships with the player's daily conditions and his or her conditions of play.

The Impoverished at Play: Assessing the Technomasculine

Such work, then, can lead to the observation that gameplay experiences of poverty represent a lowering of the bar with respect to the actual costs and other economic complexities that are involved with actual slumming: that is, and with respect to Castronova, why travel to a slum (in Tahiti or elsewhere) at all when the basic cultural practices of the activity can be experienced in a digital context? While reasonable, the observation needs to be tempered with the notion that the player's act of play is not a blank slate—that is, it takes on and expresses over time a set of values associated with its relevant cultural conditions. The question of who, exactly, might be likely to associate with such activities is relevant to such analysis, and so are questions about the larger cultural forces that create the conditions for play. This and related work can bring much-needed contextual parameters for select conceptions of play explored so far.

In *Gaming at the Edge: Sexuality and Gender at the Margins of Gamer Culture* (2015), Adrienne Shaw introduces two terms coined by Ragnhild Tronstad: sameness identity and empathic identity. Sameness identity "describes a feeling that one has become or is the character (for example feeling like I am Laura Croft when playing *Tomb Raider*)."[6] Tronstad contrasts sameness identity with empathic identity, which "describes an emotional connection with the characters' experiences what is predicated on feeling separate" from the character, for example, feeling emotionally connected to Laura Croft as a separate entity. With respect to the argument offered so far, the terms are useful states that might be associated with the player's act of play: that is, sameness identity and empathic identity might be associated with moments in time not only for the purpose of analyzing play but also for the purpose of questioning how and if they might be related through action or cumulative actions. To the extent that such states can individually and collectively be associated with action significant to absolute and relative poverty, they might become evidence of a poverty theme or themes.

For example, in *Rock N' Roll Racing* the player moves into a state of relative poverty under a very particular set of conditions, which are associated with destruction and loss. Such experiences do not demand that the player experience either sameness or empathic identity, but it is the case that the states—if activated—have significantly different implications for the player in his or her acts of play. For example, with respect to sameness identity, the personalization of destruction and loss involves notions of self-destruction as a consequence of personal failure: I have lost the race; I have been destroyed; I failed to acquire the means necessary to escape an impoverished position. Such conceptions carry the weight of player action to and through the moment of loss, and in effect historicize the loss as a matter of personal record keeping. My life and/or race ended in a state of relative poverty. The experience of empathic identity creates a related but essentially dissimilar outcome: my racer's opportunities for success resulted in a state of impoverished failure. Of course, in actual practice there is no reason to assume that the player cannot—to use Murray's term—teeter between these states in the moments leading up to and following their impoverished conclusions. One might even argue that the player moves between these "identities" precisely because one sets the stage for and amplifies the consequences of the other—back and forth and to any range of possible extents. For example, one can identify with the racer as purchases are made and one can at the same time identify with the experience of purchasing upgrades. One might slip between these identities, as neither identity is necessarily stable. Key here is the notion that such vacillations are not the result of the player's descent into poverty—rather, such vacillations are a reasonable context for the descent itself.

This notion, then, returns us to the situation of the slumming individual and the various features of slumming that pull the observer into the slum even as they work to create a barrier between the observer and the observed. Understood as features of play, these subjects might be addressed for their evident formal characteristics and then to broader questions of form. That is, are there particular tropes or other recurrent manifestations in play that work to such an effect, and, if so, is there a broader gameplay rhetoric at work, one that can be associated across select titles in ways that are as revealing of the videogame form as they are of the conditions of play in a single title? The question is a trap, to the extent that it values possibilities for play over the act of play itself. The hypothetical tropes themselves are only operative when they can be associated with the player. Here, a concept like "congruence" becomes extremely useful if it can be modified slightly: rather than convey a notion of recognition between the player's socioeconomic status and the social systems represented by a videogame, it might be understood as a player's willingness to move or be moved back and forth between experiences of sameness and empathic identity, regardless of the consequential implications that these states hold for an analysis of play: that is, the player is willing to shift self-conceptions between or among select states (e.g., the states of sameness or emphatic identity) as a condition or perhaps consequence of play. One critical value of a poverty theme for such shifting is that the theme itself in its execution (the player loses) locates a point in play that can be associated with possibilities for both sameness and empathic identity.

Understood this way, the poverty theme can be seen as a stabilizing force for analyses of identity as it relates to the player's act of play—to the extent that it invites reflection on the impoverished subject even as it associates that subject with experiences that fall beyond the realm of the reasonable for the player. This observation can be related to other concepts that emerge in Shaw's writing and in particular to her engagement with ideas from Klastrup and Tosca. Shaw, writing of their findings, notes that the authors "observe that at least in online, social games, the 'way our character looks is important to us, even in cases where appearance plays no role whatsoever in the reward system of the game.'" Shaw notes that the authors "use ethnographic methods, surveys, and interviews to analyze the role of fashion in *World of Warcraft*. They find that aesthetic choices play the dual role of differentiating avatars from everyone else and displaying status and group belonging within a normative social hierarchy."[7] With respect to the experience of poverty, the "dual role" identified by Shaw can be framed with the useful concepts of same and empathic identity. That is to say, such duality is unified under a concept of relative poverty: the player in his or her attire represents a node of differentiation in a tier or stratum of poverty with respect to players with less or greater displayed worth: the aesthetic choices play a unified role in their substantiation of player possibilities with respect to raiment as it might be located in the grander and multifold spectrum of possibilities the game offers to players.

To the extent the player experiences sameness identity or empathic identity with such representations, their experience has district interpretive implications. As an extension of self, such representations carry the weight of personal selection and acquisition—of deliberate decision-making in the context of a market or markets. Under an empathic association, these choices are held at a necessary remove from the player and are complicated by the avatar's perceived individuated needs as they relate to acquisition and ornamentation. To stand in a position of noteworthy relative poverty with respect to one's class peers is a charge against the self for the player experiencing sameness identity, while it is only a logical consequence of the gameplay system for the player experiencing empathic identity. If these positions sound similar, it is because they are, and there is no reason for why a player might not move between or indeed even hold both suppositions to be true at the same time, in their act of play. However, to the extent that these perceptional experiences are occasioned by notions of poverty, they can be located in time with such perceptions as and when they become relevant to the player—should they become relevant—and there is of course no guarantee that they will. Now, the question might be asked: how might a game unfold in ways that such perceptions become likely experiences for the player in his or her act of play?

In the titles considered so far, such perceptions are linked with expanding or expanded notions of representational possibilities for play—that is to say, expanded conceptions of other characters, including players, relating to their evident capacities or their demonstrated capacities. With this awareness, the player moves toward a self-definition or empathic definition of their avatar, relevant to his or her holdings as they bear on notions of status within one or more social contexts. Such expansion does not require sameness identity or empathic identity, or limit the player's ability to shift between these states in his or her act of play. It does, however, establish a rationale for play, a trajectory that intersects with and also exceeds the questing structure. This is exceptionally relevant for titles like *Rock N' Roll Racing* and *The Lost Vikings*, where the poverty dynamic is bound up in the notion of progress itself—the player must persist in one location until they finish in the top tier of racers in *Rock N' Roll Racing*, and the player must remain geographically bound until they use the correct sequencing of Viking skills in *The Lost Vikings*. In these games, it does not matter if the player is experiencing sameness identity or empathic identity, in terms of the consequences of relative poverty. However, in *World of Warcraft*, these identities and their essential conditions do have some significance to the consequences of relative poverty, as the consequences are context-dependent for the player. There are simply more ways to be poor and to be represented as poor in *World of Warcraft* than it in these other titles.

The notion that various titles might offer a range of opportunities for absolute and relative poverty to be represented, and the related notions that such opportunities might have coincidental as well as distinct implications for sameness identity and empathic identity, underscores the notion that a poverty theme or, indeed, poverty themes might be remarkably complex in their formulation and execution. However, such complexity is itself met by the much-greater-by-comparison economic condition the player brings to his or her acts of play, so it is crucial to consider how these varied fields of experience—one extending from the game and one extending from the player—might intersect in the act of play. For example, while *World of Warcraft* may offer a number of ways to "be poor," a growing body of scholarship on the cultural identity of the gamer is exploring the notion that the player's act of play itself may be subject to fairly complicated and prescriptive notions of being that themselves have implications for a poverty theme in a game like *World of Warcraft*.

Carly Kocurek presents and develops the notion of the "technomasculine"[8] as a gender-ideal in gaming cultures in which gaming "functions as a homosocial space, a cultural enclave for young men who came to view video gaming as a place where they could cultivate and display skill and prove their own prowess and competence."[9] This view of the player's act of play as a competition with relevance to egotistical male striving is further qualified by Kocurek as relating to "knowledge and intelligence, fierce competitiveness and independence, and a willingness to disregard rules and standards, these boyish early adopters survive and excel by showing themselves particularly adept at playing by the emergent standards of a society in flux."[10] This noting of a gaming archetype that, itself, emerges from views on gaming cuts a bright line across many of the comments offered by Murray, Galloway, and Castronova, to the extent it reinforces the idea that gaming shapes and is shaped by distinct cultural focus that, collectively, endow the act of play with particular meaning(s). Without dismissing Kocurek's conception of the technomasculine—which is persuasive and sound—we might ask how this cultural construct works to facilitate or otherwise delimit the economic experiences that are availed to players in their various acts of play. For example, in the context of Kocurek's technomasculine, relative poverty is understood not only in the immediacy of the player's act of play, but in the context of broader competitive awareness—that is, with an awareness of the manifold opportunities for play that exist outside of the player's own experience and against which the player must strive to make a mark by showing dominance of the gaming space.

This observation complicates many of the points I have offered above, to the extent it re-frames the player's acts of play as occurring in a specified context—the technomasculine—which is itself laden with economic anxieties with implications for the player as he or she comes to an act of play. With respect to *Rock N' Roll Racing*, *The Lost Vikings*, and *World of Warcraft*, the question now becomes how relative poverty might be prioritized with respect to the technomasculine: that is, does—or, more usefully, can—the technomasculine shape the experience of relative poverty?

As it is presented and defined by Kocurek, the concept would seem to function in part as a pre-determined value for relative poverty—that is, the player comes to the game in a context where relative poverty is understood—at least partially—in the context of the technomasculine, with its associated concerns related to competition. To experience relative poverty in such a scenario is to fall away from—but still be accounted for under—the expectations of the technomasculine.

This view has additional implications for how relative poverty might be perceived in play, to the extent that persistence in a state of relative poverty is seemingly at odds with the technomasculine—as the impoverished player is not in a position to show his or her dominance over his or her peers. However, that relevance is particular and can be understood with a comparison between *Rock N' Roll Racing*, *The Lost Vikings*, and *World of Warcraft*. In *Rock N' Roll Racing*, the player's ability to demonstrate creative rule breaking/bending and dominance is limited to their ability to navigate tracks with their pressing dangers, so that they end the race in the top tier. The path to victory may come with a range of possible decisions, but the ultimate goal is certain and obtainable. A similar situation arises in *The Lost Vikings*, as the player is free to exert several minor possible choices to accelerate or otherwise define victory, but the path to victory is itself clear. However, in *World of Warcraft*, there is no persistent state of victory, as the quest system and expanding geography of the game are forever moving the literal goalposts of play further from the player's achievements. With respect to the technomasculine, the concept would seem to be most significant to games that provided the most opportunities for players to move up and into positions of quantifiable dominance over other players. However, what happens with the markers of success are far from definite—that is, what happens in a game where there is no clear end state, or if there is such a state it is routinely turned over and expanded upon with additional game content, such as in the case in titles like *World of Warcraft*?

This possibility suggests that the technomasculine might be as relevant to individual in-game accomplishments as it is to total game dominance, and this relevance has special meaning for conceptions of relative poverty—and poverty in general—in gameplay. In the context of technomasculine, relative poverty works to set immediate goalposts for player advancement: to move to a representation that elevates the player in his or her act of play over others in an instance of play in what is already an affirmation of the technomasculine. In this way, relative poverty might be subsumed by the technomasculine and contribute to meaning making in ways that also exceed the concepts of sameness identity and empathic identity. That is to say, the player's acceptance of multiple or contrasting identity positions is, in such an instance, all in the service of a larger adherence to and affirmation of the technomasculine.

Representing Impoverished Communities in Videogames

While the technomasculine can be considered as a contextualizing force for a poverty thematic, it is important to note that the phenomenon itself has evident limitations in its associations with poverty thematics, generally. This is because the drive to establish progressive and/or tiered orderings of player accomplishments is descriptive of and attentive to movements toward victory, and while the threat of relative poverty haunts all such orderings in the technomasculine, the threat itself stands as a condition that is to be avoided and/or, at most, detested if it is otherwise unavoidable. What is not accounted for under the technomasculine is the experience of seeking our and/or otherwise reveling in an impoverished state. Or, to be more precise, the act of willfully persisting in—or simply prolonging experiences within—a persistent state of relative poverty is anathema to the technomasculine. This limitation is significant, particularly with the concept of slumming considered so far, as slumming as such represents a strong desire to do exactly that—to marry the experience of play with the experience of what is essentially a consequence-free impoverishment. Understood in this way, useful conceptual boundaries can be established for both concepts, at least with respect to how they might be related to one another: the technomasculine can account for relative poverty as long as relative poverty functions as a whip crack near the ear, driving the player "upwards" and "away" from the experience of relative want. At the same time, relative poverty squares with the technomasculine to the extent that poverty stands as a threat for play, but one that is infinitely divisible in ways that established increasingly more specific layers of apparent success or failure for the player at play.

This boundary for association can lead to the observation that the player's act of play might at the same time represent an investment in moving away from certain experiences of relative want while also representing an investment in moving toward alternative stages and experiences of relative want and desire. Arguably, this experience is relevant to title like *World of*

Warcraft—that is, the player is always finding him or herself to be inferior to the standards for survival in yet another social system. The player's act of play in such a game has as its core the experience of impoverishment. It is a strange impoverishment to be sure, just as the slumming of nineteenth-century adventures found strangeness in the spectacle of poverty at a remove, but like slumming it conveys a central conceit, which is that poverty is an elective experience, which can be experienced at a remove and at will. The technomasculine affirms (redeems) this fantasy with paths to virtual wealth that are ready to be explored and exploited by payers if they have the will and skill to master the game's secret byways to contextual achievements. The relationship between these concepts can be understood as one form of the general teetering identified by Murray. The player moves back and forth from positions of accomplishments to positions of implied status, back and forth with a regularity that almost implies harmony. Poverty is not "a" game in a title like *World of Warcraft*. Poverty is "the" game.

Such play is relevant to other titles from Blizzard Entertainment, perhaps most obviously to the *StarCraft* and *Diablo* franchises, even though these titles do not occur within persistent worlds. *StarCraft*'s development in the mid-1990s was led by Chris Metzen and James Phinney, who also worked to develop the game's premise and narrative structure. In broad strokes, the game involves a series of escalating conflicts between humans and two alien races, the insectoid Zergs and the powerfully and looming Protoss. As the title suggests, *StarCraft* shares a number of features with *Warcraft: Orcs & Humans* and *Warcraft II: Tides of Darkness*. The player moves through a series of maps in pursuit of larger goals of domination, and over the course of the game has the opportunity to play as all of the major races represented in the game. With respect to relative poverty, the concept can be understood in much the same way as relative poverty in the *Warcraft II: Tides of Darkness* and *Warcraft: Orcs & Humans*. Players who fail to achieve the means and methods for advancement fail to advance in the course of the single player game. In terms of the game's player versus player scenarios, such failure is not necessarily significant to geography, as the player can choose to simply play in another area. However, loss is indicated by the consumption of one player's major resources by the other, an act that radically reduces the losing player's economic possibilites over time. In short, in these titles the poverty theme has the added feature of incremental economic destruction—you get to see yourself become more and more impoverished with respect to the foe or foes against which you are playing. To the extent that the game dramatizes economic destruction, it—and also *Warcraft: Orcs & Humans* and *Warcraft II: Tides of Darkness*—presents a distinct dimension to the poverty theme, at least when it is considered in light of *Rock N' Roll Racing* and *The Lost Vikings*. In those titles, the economic diminution over time is relevant to play, but only in a minor sense—loss is dramatic in the tally of the racers in *Rock N' Roll Racing*, or encroaching in *The Lost Vikings* in the sense of diminished and limited lives for each of the three Vikings. In the real time strategy titles, the balance of economic possibilites establishes a shifting contexts for the evident standards for living—as one player or faction becomes more powerful, the other must work to match and eventually exceed that potential, or become victim to economic disparity. This essential feature of play also distinguishes these games from *World of Warcraft*, a game in which economic diversity is never necessarily pressing—that is, one might strive to meet or exceed the holdings of one or more players, or to meet or exceed the holdings that are generally necessary to advance within a given environment, but simple existence and persistence is not necessarily forbidden if one fails in this way—one can always simply move away from the adventure that is too challenging, one can always simply observe economic disparity and not become a victim to it. This option is not an option in the *StarCraft* and Real-Time Strategy *Warcraft* titles. The rhythms of these games are tied to the rise and fall of economic forces and financial positioning.

Taken together, these notions lead to the observation that the relevance of a poverty theme to the player's act of play is highly contextual and that gameplay variations are as significant for such themes as are the various contexts that bring the player to an act of play in the first place. Notions of contextuality can and do raise meaningful questions about significance—that is, if and when a poverty theme is identified, is it the case that the theme itself has significance beyond its own manifestation in play? This and related questions move the conversation that has been established so far into broader questions of meaning and meaning making. For example, considered as a feature of the technomasculine, a poverty theme would have proscribed meaning—that is, it would be in the service of the technomasculine. However, considered apart from the technomasculine or some other necessarily redemptive gameplay value, a poverty theme would essentially stand on its own, with respect to notions of purpose. The same is essentially true if the theme is divorced from prescriptive notions of form: that is, the notion that poverty themes are simply an anatomical reality of the videogame form. A less proscriptive but equal relevant concern would be the notion that poverty themes have gameplay pedigrees—that is, the idea that there are play traditions that formulate and express related and/or otherwise relatable poverty themes, and that such expressions have an artistic or simply crass commercial context. Rather than proceed under a grand notion of poverty theme meaning or meanings—rather than attempt to discern their collective implications—the goal in what follows will be to regard and explore such gameplay phenomena for their possible associations with the player at play, to elevate as much as possible the human subjects that become associated with such themes.

With respect to game studies, such work can begin with a consideration of the discursive practices that have developed around the discipline for the purpose of expanding academic participation. This may seem like an idiosyncratic place to begin consideration of the human subject as it might be related to videogames. However, and as might have been inferred from arguments in this and previous chapters, game studies' contributions to the academy are often—though not exclusively—contributions that reach out from the discipline for the purpose of engaging with scholarship from some related—or relatable—field. It is an interdisciplinary enterprise: select publications associated with game studies growth and development have, as shall be considered, a vested and by now long-standing interest in facilitating interdisciplinary conversations. Indeed, investment in such conversations can be characterized as having more relevance to the field than efforts to define the field with discipline-specific insights. That is not to say that such efforts have not been undertaken—they are undertaken even now. Yet, it is to say that forays into the player's act of play tend to arrive with a specific, field-related value—or perhaps the term "imperative" is more accurate—which is to first and foremost create an interdisciplinary connection that goes on to produce a meaningful insight into such or related subjects. The following chapter will consider such practices and their bearing on the argument at hand.

Notes

1. Murray, Chapter 4.
2. Ibid.
3. Galloway, "Social Realism."
4. Castronova, *Synthetic*, 80.
5. Ibid., 2112.

6. Shaw, *Gaming*, 100–01.
7. Ibid., 136.
8. Kocurek, 160.
9. Kocurek 3375.
10. Ibid., 2570.

Bibliography

Murray, Janet H. *Hamlet on the Holodeck: The Future of Narrative in Cyberspace*. Free Press, 1997. Kindle edition.

Shaw, Adrienne. *Gaming at the Edge: Sexuality and Gender at the Margins of Gamer Culture*. Minneapolis: University of Minnesota Press, 2015. Kindle edition.

CHAPTER 4

The Player and Game Studies' Rhetoric of Inclusion

The Player's Acts of Play: Identity in Gaming Cultures

While the technomasculine stands poised to redeem select poverty thematics and/or the experience of relative poverty, it is arguably dependent on such experiences and represents cultural practices for valuing and, frankly, capitalizing on their associated anxieties. Such practices are not necessarily called for by a poverty thematic or thematics, and this observation can lead to questions about alternative valuations for play that might be associated with conceptions and expressions of relative poverty. Such concerns can be aligned with recent criticism and commentary concerned with identity in gaming cultures. A short list of recent works that take up or otherwise advance academic perspectives on this area of interest could include Alenda P. Chang's *Playing Nature: Ecology in Video Games*, Marcus Maloney et al.'s *Gender, Musculinity, and Video Gaming*, and Brendan Keogh's *A Play of Bodies*. While these critics offer distinct theses substantiated with divergent analytical and methodological considerations, their arguments are bound by a common concern: the relevance of player identity to a player's acts of play. Of the three works, *Playing Nature* approaches the subject from what is arguably the broadest perspective. Chang's consideration of ecological contexts for play elevates notions of player identity in manifold systems of interdependence delimited by select resources and opportunities for resource management. Her work established novel

A. Crowley, *Representations of Poverty in Videogames*,
https://doi.org/10.1007/978-3-031-00144-4_4

contexts for considering and valuing the player at play. The need for such criticism is anticipated by Maloney et al. Their argument explores how online communities like those found on Reddit can become hostile to open discourse on identity and its relevance to the player's act of play. Maloney et al.'s argument might be aligned with Chang's to advance the notion that games are populated by players with diverse and perhaps irreconcilable socioeconomic agendas, which may be as relevant to their acts of play as the very models of interdependence that structure a game's ecological systems. The intersection of such models and players is at the heart of Keogh's text, which begins with a recognition that movement into and out of virtual spaces comes with associated notions of estrangement—of a need to articulate how the individual player might reconcile his or her own perceptions with the game's presented world with how the presented world is supposedly perceived by the characters that are represented in that world.

This and related work emerge in the aftermath of efforts to locate what Carly A. Kocurek calls the cultural identity of video gamer.[1] Related efforts from Adrienne Shaw and Shira Chess take a special interest in the significance of gender to the player's act of play. For example, Shaw's consideration of representation extends to notions of identification and the relevance of identification to the formation of cultural notions of who is and who is not permitted to be a gamer. The notion that such permissions have taken shape—sometimes deliberately and sometimes perhaps simply by cultural consequence—is explored by Kocurek, who considers in detail the socioeconomic forces bearing on the videogame arcade and the consequences of those forces for both boys and girls over time, with respect to notions of equality in access and parity in play. For her part, Chess' attention to the essential estrangement that awaits women in such spaces extends to the topic of character interactions—and how sexism in games can both define and destroy possibilities for plays in ways that can fundamentally taint gaming models, particularly when notions of interdependence are at stake. This work represents a well-defined culmination of an early twenty-first-century thinking on videogames and gaming cultures, and it also sets a bright line standard for how the discipline might advance in productive ways in future scholarship waves.

To the extent that these and related titles foreground questions bearing on the intersection of identity and gaming in modern markets, they can be connected with a notifiable shift in game studies scholarship that can be centered on the period of the Global Great Recession (2007–2009). At the level of monograph, the period marks a movement away from broad questions bearing on the videogame form itself. Previously considered works, such as Janet H. Murray's *Hamlet on the Holodeck: The Future of Narrative in Cyberspace*, Edmund Castronova's *Synthetic Worlds: The Business and Culture of Online Games*, and Ian Bogost's *Persuasive Games: The Expressive Power of Videogames*, are suggestive of that period's form-centered investigations. For example, Murray's effort to address computational technologies arrives at a time before significant work on gaming cultures has been initiated. The same can be said of Castronova's extended consideration of economics and videogames in 2005, which emerged without a specific understanding of the gamer or player as a discrete subject determined by powerful cultural and subcultural characteristics, a rhetorical characteristic the text shares with Bogost's *Persuasive Games.* Certainly, this is not a shortcoming in any of these arguments, as the authors were operating in a critical landscape that is quite different from the one Shaw, Kocurek, and Chess would inhabit a decade or so later and which we all—arguably—inhabit now.

With respect to the issue of identity, the critical movement from Murray to Kocurek might be traced through several titles that take up issues of identity as part of a broader commentary on class and economics, several of which we have already considered in some detail. For example, it can be located in Jesper Juul's *Half-Real: Video Games Between Real Worlds and Fictional Rules*, Edward Castronova's *Exodus to the Virtual World: How Online Fun Is Changing Reality*, Nick Dyer-Witheford and Greig de Peuter's *Games of Empire: Global Capitalism and Video Games*, and Randi Nichols' *The Video Game Business.* Juul's consideration of "real rules and fictional worlds" turns at multiple points toward the subject of economics,[2] but generally only for the purpose of noting that economic theory is just beyond the boundaries of a critical analysis of videogames. However, in turn, the author advances the notion that economics is generally relevant to the gaming industry and the notion that a specific economic analysis of the player's act of play can establish a critical boundary for analysis. That boundary is drawn in some detail in works like Castronova's *Exodus to the Virtual World.* At multiple points in his argument, Castronova recognizes that economic and public policies shape the player's act of play, and these comments serve as context for his eventual comments on the significance of in-game capital to the player's act of play, a notion that leads him to observe the relevance of poverty to a large number of online titles: poverty being a key feature of the player's starting position and also a recurring experience as the player advances toward one goal or another.[3] The relevance of economic policy to the gaming industry and, through that, to the player's act of play is a central concern for Dyer-Witheford and de Peuter, who attend to a so-called fractured economic order to describe the growth and development of the videogame industry, which they view as part of a larger late-capitalist disaster with planetary implications.[4] As we have seen, these concerns lead them to their early and intriguing comments on "virtual poverty" and "actual poverty."[5] They note that while "virtual poverty" can be experienced in titles like *Second Life*, actually playing *Second Life* requires a computer and a broadband connection, which "limits access to the upper percentiles of global wealth."

Consider as such, game studies can be regarded as a field with coherent and extended interests that move out from and generally back to particular conceptions of the player at play: for example, the formal as well as broader conditions of play that are either inextricable from play or temporally relevant to play. Such work has often found itself gesturing toward economic concerns—detailed or otherwise—though it has rarely found itself to be accounted for by such concerns. One possible explanation for the field's long-standing interest in such matters is the evident relationship between relative poverty and the player's act of play: not only as it might be realized within a title but, rather, as a phenomenon that occurs and recurs in ways that suggest experiential differences between games and, more importantly, between players.

Contexts for Play: Identity and Poverty

While some works make light to moderate use of economic theory to account for the formation of the "video gamer" identity, such commentary is less relevant to the identified work by Shaw and Chess: it does not find an explicit expression in the reasoning. This is, of course, not a shortcoming of either argument, as each argument has its own aims and methodologies. However, and largely because of Kocurek's success with the subject, it is reasonable to ask how Shaw's consideration of representation might be expanded with attention to the relevance of economics to the player's act of play and also how Chess' commentary on virtual estrangement might be elaborated on with a consideration of economics and poverty and their relevance to the same. The notion that such work might have broader relevance can be inferred from a number of publications that approach notions of class consciousness in popular videogames published by companies such as Blizzard Entertainment (e.g., Snodgrass (2016), Pearce (2017)), Rockstar Games (Stark (2010) and Spring (2015)) and BioWare (Geraci (2014), Krobová (2015), and Hayden (2017)).

Snodgrass et al., building on the work of Nick Yee's commentary on the motivational factors for understanding play in massively multiplayer online games, conclude that "culturally sensitive measures" better predict problematic factors of play, pointing to the important role of "sociocultural online play."[6] While the work itself says very little about economics or poverty, the question of economic insecurity is represented in the author's survey of players, and one of the larger implications of the argument is that economics and economic insecurity are one of the "culturally sensitive measures" that might be pursued to gain greater insight into the player's act of play in titles like *World of Warcraft*. A related notion emerges in Alyssa Maria Pearce's "Exploring Performance of Gendered Identity" in *World of Warcraft*. Pearce's observation of gendered stereotypes in the game's chat logs raises questions about how these comments and types of comments might be addressed with "culturally sensitive measures."[7] While the article does not suggest a specific path forward for analysis, the recognition of stereotypes as being significant to the player's social context in gaming environments underscores a need to understand how such contexts share in and are shaped by the act of play itself. Marcel Martoncik and Jan Loksa's "Do *World of Warcraft* (MMORPG) Players Experience Less Loneliness and Social Anxiety in Online World (Virtual Environment) than in Real World (Offline)?" moves in a similar direction, in that the authors note a condition of play—that is, a decrease in reported "loneliness" for players that are contextualized by their sociocultural condition, even if the authors do not offer a specific understanding of how and why it is that these same conditions shape players experiences of loneliness in their acts of play.[8] Each of these titles summons to mind the relevance of class to the player's act of play, in ways that compel further inquiry that stretches beyond the list of academic sources any of these authors cite in the course of their various arguments. An alignment and consideration of this literature illuminates novel opportunities for addressing representations of class and socioeconomic status—and in particular impoverished communities—within select videogame titles.

The critical possibilities suggested by an alignment and association of such and related scholarship hold unexplored significance for another, post-Great Recession movement within game studies: the investigation of aesthetic traditions with relevance to the player's act of play in digital environments. At the level of monograph, early work on this subject can be found in titles as diverse as Tamer Thabet's *Video Game Narrative and Criticism: Playing the Story* (2015), Souvik Mukherjee's *Video Games and Storytelling: Reading Games and Playing Books* (2015), Timothy J. Welsh's *Mixed Realism: Videogames and the Violence of Fiction* (2017), and Darshana Jayemanne's *Performativity in Art, Literature, and Videogames* (2017). Welsh's consideration of the various and potential factors that may impact how players interact with communication devices traces out an extended consideration of postmodern aesthetics in literary works from the end of the twentieth century and leads him to the observation that "wired culture is a mixed reality, conducted as exchanges between virtual and material contexts."[9] This leads him to the observation that "Mixed realism describes the ways media-generated virtualities reframe or recontextualize the real-world activity of interacting with them."[10] The notion here then is that the gaming experience itself has implications for the player and his or her acts of play—to the extent that the act does not—to borrow a term from Galloway—simply "transliterate" the context of the player into the experience of the game.[11] This tension is also expressed in Dyer-Witheford and de Peuter's comments on the distinctions between real and virtual poverty: for example, the act of game playing itself functionally removes the player from an association with poverty as it is experienced by the globe's truly impoverished. Jayemanne expresses a related notion when asserting that "A Videogame can be seen as an archive that is accessed, modified, and manipulated in a very particular way: playful performance."[12] Harkening back to Juul's distinction between real rules and fictional worlds, the concept of playful performance foregrounds the structural limitations of the player's act of play—which both limits and qualifies the values of play, at least with respect to the act of play itself in the context of the videogame.

Welsh's and Jayemanne's efforts to articulate a theory or theories for describing the relevance of context-specific qualifications to or for the player's acts of play move toward a theory of addressing, for example, virtual poverty—to the extent that notions of poverty can be reconciled with "mixed reality" and performativity. With respect to "mixed reality," Welsh attends to the ways in which videogames seek to mediate the experience of poverty, much as global poverty is mediated by first world nations for their citizens: it encourages us to think about the subject even though it divorces us from the subject. Jayemanne does not take on the concept of economics or poverty directly, but the author does address in some detail the notion of class, and how it is relevant to the player's performativity in play and also to the possibilities for performance in titles that use class-based systems to shape the player's experiences and opportunities for expression.[13] Here too what is being recognized is an unequal intersection of real-world circumstances with the experience of classed possibilities for play, an act that moves the player into a new economic context that may relate to but which is also fundamentally to be distinguished from the player's own context.

As is evident in both Welsh and Jayemanne, "mixed reality" and "performativity" are evidence of a phenomenon, but they are not wholly descriptive of that phenomenon. Indeed, both texts position themselves as efforts to bring essential awareness to the open question of how the player's act of play shapes and is shaped by the contexts of player and played (player and game). It is an open question if such shaping might be described with something like a unified theory of gaming, but just because the question is open that does not mean that it is particularly desirable. Efforts to express or approach unified understandings of videogames are the shovelware of modern gaming criticism, and the history of the field's development suggests greater critical rewards lie in bounded considerations of play, rather than in totalizing pronouncements with diminishing critical returns. Or, to put it another way, the critical possibilities at hand are vast, and scholarship that recognizes this essential notion is perhaps, in our common moment, quite desirable, as it stands to unlock passageways for future work, rather than obscure novel insights from the field's newest, most vulnerable voices.

Before approaching these possibilities, it is useful to review and consider evidence of how game studies–related publications have worked to create space for interdisciplinary considerations of games, gamers, and gaming. Such evidence can be found in the mission statements and citation records of three noteworthy, field-related publications: *Game Studies: The International Journal of Computer Games Research*, *First Person Scholar*, and *Not Your Mama's Gamer*. While this review will take us away from the concept of poverty momentarily, the academic trends that will be illuminated by the review will be crucial for our continuing considerations of the subject and its relevance to the player's acts of play. Context for this review and its findings can be located in Jesper Juul's *Half-Real: Video Games Between Real Rules and Fictional Worlds* (2005). There, and as mentioned at the beginning of this book, Juul reflects on the development of game and videogame studies in the second half of the twentieth century and observes that the early twenty-first century "has been something of a gold rush and a race [for scholars to] point out special aspects of games, to format the field, to define words, and to point to similarities and dissimilarities between games and other cultural forms." The concept of economics and, more specifically, poverty has played a role in that "gold rush." A review of citation practices relevant to scholars racing to define the field during the first and second decades of the twenty-first century reveals how and in some cases perhaps even why a concept like poverty should be expected to have had general and perhaps only general relevance to the field for a number of years—perhaps too many years.

A Struggle for Definition: *Game Studies: The International Journal of Computer Games Research*

Game Studies: The International Journal of Computer Games Research underwent a landing page modification in the mid-2000s that is relevant to current conversations around the field and its ongoing development, such as those that have been occurring around the concept of poverty. Launched in July 2001, the journal maintained a stable site description and mission statement on its landing page until December 2006. At that time, both the site description and mission statement underwent minor but noteworthy modifications. I'll be reviewing and analyzing these modifications with a framework derived from Philip E. Smith's "The Mission of Rhetoric and the Rhetoric of Mission Statements" (1998) and then associating my findings with the role of Janet H. Murray's *Hamlet on the Holodeck: The Future of Narrative in Cyberspace* (1997) in the journal's citation record for 2001 through 2006. My findings detail how Murray's text was deployed by a range of scholars in ways that cohere with the journal's original and modified site descriptions and mission statements. Murray's text has been selected for consideration on the basis of its special relevance to the syntax of the journal's mission statement and also on the basis of the frequency with which *Hamlet on the Holodeck* is cited during the period in question. It is one of the only three texts to be cited in more than one of the journal's initial five volumes. It is matched only by Espen Aarseth's *Cybertext: Perspectives on Ergodic Literature* (1997), at three out of five volumes. J.C. Hertz's *Joystick Nation: How Videogames Gobbled Our Money, Won Our Hearts and Rewired Our Minds* (1997) comes in third with two of five volume mentions. As a touchstone for the field,

Hamlet on the Holodeck functionally drew together interdisciplinary perspectives, many of which adopted or otherwise endorsed key concepts from Murray's arguments. However, these adoptions and endorsements did not themselves lead to associated specifications of concepts or concerns from the relevant interdisciplinary fields. This patterning is similar to the role of poverty in the various monographs explored in Chap. 1, to the extent that, in those documents, poverty emerges without evident discipline-specific qualifications.

To begin, between July 2001 and October 2006, *Game Studies* published five volumes containing seven total issues. The landing page for each issue features the following site description and mission statement in its top left corner, a prominent spot that made the passages hard to overlook. The site description and mission read as follows:

> Game Studies is a crossdisciplinary journal dedicated to games research, web-published several times a year at www.gamestudies.org. Our primary focus is aesthetic, cultural and communicative aspects of computer games.
>
> Our mission—To explore the rich cultural genre of games; to give scholars a peer-reviewed forum for their ideas and theories; to provide an academic channel for the ongoing discussions on games and gaming.[14]

With respect to the question of to whom these passages are addressed, Espen Aarseth offers the following in the editorial he contributed to the journal's launch issue. He writes:

> 2001 ... has seen the first international scholarly conference on computer games, in Copenhagen in March. ... 01-02 may also be the academic year when regular graduate programs in computer game studies are offered for the first time in universities. And it *might* be the first time scholars and academics take computer games seriously, as a cultural field whose value is hard to overestimate.[15]

Aarseth's use of "may also" and "might" underscore the notion that the publication anticipates an audience that did not yet exist could be assumed in for the near future. In a recent editorial on the subject of the journal's now twenty-year history, Aarseth clarifies and specifies this concern, writing,

> Starting the journal was an easy decision. ... The Digital Art and Culture [DAC] conferences, which were held for the first time in Bergen in 1998 and in Atlanta the following year, demonstrated a clearly growing, multidis-

> ciplinary body of games research. The DAC conference series became the main recruiting and strategizing venue for the birth of the journal.[16]

From these passages, then, one can conclude that the Digital Art and Culture conference participants are part of the journal's assumed audience in 2001 and that the original site description and mission statement are crafted in such a way so as to be of interest to that audience and the kinds of audiences that might spin out of such organizations.

The language used to reach out to these potential readers/contributors is interesting and, I'd argue, relevant to the site's early citation record, at least as it might be characterized by the presence of Janet Murray and, to a lesser degree, Espen Aarseth. Philip E. Smith reflects on some 300 mission statements, pulled from a range of English departments in North American colleges and universities. Smith's engagement with these documents leads him to some general observations about mission statements in higher education, most notably the advice that such statements attend to three theoretical modes, which he describes as, first, "the specialized rhetoric of disciplinary insiders," next "the rhetoric of academic inquiry," and finally "public rhetoric that best serves to address audiences outside our disciplines and institutions."[17] With respect to the first rhetoric—the rhetoric of disciplinary insiders—Smith intends concepts and concerns generally held by scholars in a particular field. The second rhetoric, the rhetoric of academic inquiry, is envisioned as interdisciplinary and as extending from general notions of advanced scholarship. Finally, with "public rhetoric," Smith conveys the notion of a rhetoric that extends from a general population, one that is not necessarily conversant with the conventions of academic discourse.

Under the lens of Smith's terms, the first passage in the journal's 2001 self-description might be understood as follows: it draws from and makes significant use of the rhetoric of academic inquiry. Terms and phrases like "crossdisciplinary journal," "primary focus," "research," and "aesthetic, cultural, and communicative aspects" have ready and special associations with the work of academic research. At the same time, it can be concluded that the passage has little to offer with respect to notions of disciplinary insiders if we envision disciplinary insiders as game studies scholars: other than to name games research and computer games in the passage. That is to say, it does not offer any technical terms or concepts specific to the discipline itself, other than games. With respect to public discourse, there is limited phrasing here. On the whole, then, we might say this language is directed at academic insiders, which certainly makes sense for a self-described "crossdisciplinary journal" centered on an assumedly expanding field of inquiry.

When we turn to the second passage, the mission, similar observations can be made, but with an important caveat:

> Our mission—To explore the rich cultural genre of games; to give scholars a peer-reviewed forum for their ideas and theories; to provide an academic channel for the ongoing discussions on games and gaming.

Here too again one might note the presence of language specific to academic insiders: "rich cultural genre" of games, "scholars," "peer-reviewed forum," "ideas and theories," and "academic channel," all work to that effect. And, here, too, again, there is a lack of discourse specific to disciplinary insiders and a general lack of public discourse. Again, the lack of such discourse is not surprising, given, as Aarseth explains, the founders' assumption that the discipline was anticipated but not yet manifested within the academy.

However, it is important to note how the language specific to academic inquiry is coded to communicate a reference relevant to disciplinary insiders, such as they might have existed in 2001—and assumedly associated with the DAC. To see that code, it is important to know that Janet H. Murray's *Hamlet on the Holodeck: The Future of Narrative in Cyberspace* (1997) is a noteworthy subject-specific publication that preceded the emergence of the journal by approximately four years. The relevance of that text to the inaugural issue of *Game Studies* can be inferred from the reference listings of three of the total four essays that are included in the issue, which cite the document. Indeed, that document remained one of the most frequently cited documents in the journal through 2008.

In her monograph—and as is perhaps already evident from the title—Murray makes extensive use of *Star Trek: The Next Generation* as a cultural context for understanding the storytelling capacities of computational technologies, like videogames, and uses the concept of the Holodeck as a metaphor for how we might engage with videogames in the then-coming millennium. The coding of the journal's mission statement invokes the syntax of the *Star Trek* Enterprise's famous mission statement—included at the beginning of the original *Star Trek* series and *Star Trek: The Next Generation* which reads as follows:

> Space: the final frontier. These are the voyages of the starship *Enterprise*. Its five-year mission: to explore strange new worlds. To seek out new life and new civilizations. To boldly go where no man has gone before!

The mission of *Game Studies* borrows heavily from the syntax of the Enterprise's mission, to an extent that suggests the authors are intentionally alluding to the program. For instance, the *Game Studies* statement begins with the term "mission" and then follows that term with three "to" statements. The first such statement even makes use of the same verb "explore" that is found in the Enterprise statement.

In 2006, the *Game Studies* landing page underwent a minor but arguably meaningful transformation: the mission statement was elevated in visibility above the site description, and the site description was developed with elaborations. These changes can generally be associated with Smith's rhetoric of academic inquiry. The changes are as follows:

> Game Studies is a non-profit, open-access, crossdisciplinary journal dedicated to games research, web-published several times a year at www.gamestudies.org.

"Non-profit" might be associated with "public discourse," as it is not particular to academic communities, but "open-access" can be associated with the rhetoric of academic inquiry. Other language was also added:

> Our primary focus is aesthetic, cultural and communicative aspects of computer games, but any "previously unpublished article" focused on games and gaming is welcome. "Proposed articles" should be "jargon-free," and should attempt to "shed new light" on games, rather than simply use games as "metaphor or illustration of some other theory or phenomenon."

Here the new phrasing offers nothing that is evidently specific to the discipline, and the language is also too specific to academic enterprises to be considered "public discourse." One observation here is that the 2006 modification retained and expanded on the academic rhetoric that was so important to the original 2001 statement. At the same time, the editors found no need to return to and expand upon the parody syntax of the mission statement.

One all too obvious conclusion that might be reached here is that the editors have retained—and doubled down on—the original mission language, as the language is unchanged but the statement's visibility has been elevated. This observation can lead to the question of why the language was so significant to the editors. It should be noted here that *Star Trek* itself is not a subject of inquiry identified in any of the journal's issues over the past twenty years, at the level of the essay title. So why is it so relevant to the mission statement? Is there an answer beyond idiosyncratic behavior on the part of the journal's founders? The role of Murray's text in the citation record is one possible answer—her text functions as a—and arguably *the*—significant touchstone for interdisciplinary perspectives on games in the journal in the 2001–2006 period. It is the framework that makes "ongoing discussions" of games possible (along with Aarseth's *Cybertext*) in the inaugural period.

During that time, Murray's work is cited in the following essays: Marie-Laurie Ryan's "Beyond Myth and Metaphor: The Case of Narrative in Digital Media"; Jesper Juul's "Games Telling Stories?"; Markku Eskelinen's "The Gaming Situation"; Torill Mortensen's "Playing with Player's Potential: Methodologies for Muds"; Helen W. Kennedy's "Laura Croft: Feminist Icon or CyberBimbo: On the Limits of Textual Analysis"; Diane Carr's "Play Dead: Genre and Affect in *Silent Hill* and *Planescape Torment*"; Julian Kucklich's "Perspectives on Computer Game Philology"; and Laurie Taylor's "When Seams Fall Apart Video Game Space and the Player." With respect to the original site description and mission statement, Murray's citation record leads to the following observations. The involved authors represent a range of disciplines, at the level of their credentialing at the time of their work's publication. Ryan is identified as an independent scholar with a PhD in French; Juul is identified as a PhD student in computer games with an MA in Nordic literature; Eskelinen is identified as having attained *candidatus philolagiae* in comparative literature; Mortensen is identified as holding a master's degree in Media Theory; and Carr is identified as a videogames researcher. Kenncy is not presented with an academic attribution, but presented with an academic ranking. In the context of these credentials, Murray's text serves as a common discipline-specific document—it is literally what draws these arguments together at the level of citation. As might be inferred from the small number of works that are cross-referenced in the journal's inaugural period, points of academic convergence at the level of citation are *the exception* rather than the rule in the journal's essays.

At the same time, it is important to note that while these authors are engaged with *Hamlet on the Holodeck*, they are not as a cohort engaged with any particular ideas or notions in the text. For the sake of expediency,

I'll note that *Hamlet on the Holodeck* is broken into an introduction and ten subsequent chapters. Five of the seven authors cite work from "Chapter 5: Agency," but these citations do not intersect on specific pages or over specific ideas in that chapter. Ryan is engaged with the introduction and Chapter 10; Juul is engaged with the introduction, and then Eskelinen, Mortensen, Kennedy, Carr, and Kucklich are engaged with Chapter 5. With the exception of Ryan, these engagements are non-critical engagements—they apply a concept from Murray to the author's argument without interrogating or qualifying the cited passage or passages: for example, Juul draws an assumption from Murray—the assumption that there is "a promising future for digital storytelling." Eskelinen references Murray's cultural analysis of *Tetris.* Mortensen presents Murray's definition of "agency." Kennedy draws on the term "symbolic drama" and applies it to her argument. Carr presents Murray's conception of "the solvable maze and the tangled rhizome," and *Kucklich* presents Murray's term "interactive narrative." The citation record here, then, shows us attention to and endorsements of select terms and phrases from Murray.

This is significant because such passages indicate academic interest but they do not build something like a disciplinary-specific perspective on the identified ideas—that is, the works do not interrogate the identified concepts for the purpose of clarification or qualification. This too is in keeping with the journal's essential mission, to the extent that it can be understood as an effort to draw academic fields to an awareness of games and not necessarily to a point where such fields begin to interrogate scholarship on games.

The 2006 modifications to *Game Studies* landing page affirm the journal's then expressed commitment to cultivating academic interest in games and games research. The affirmation and elevation of the original mission, with its Murray-specific coding, underscores the continuing relevance of what was, in 2001, merely the assumed relevance of *Hamlet on the Holodeck* to the journal's citation record. That record indicates academics from a range of fields found terms and concepts in the text that facilitated their arguments on games and games research. These deployments are generally associated with Murray's comments on agency and are generally speaking non-critical endorsements.

Murray's citation record can be associated with the other major work deployed in the journal's launch period, Espen Aarseth's *Cybertext: Perspectives on Ergodic Literature.* It is deployed by many of the same authors, in many of the same essays: Ryan, Juul, Eskelinen, Mortensen,

Carr, and Kucklich all reference the text, as do Newman, Frasca, and Galloway. Aarseth and Murray are generally (with the exception of Ryan) uncritically endorsed in these references, and these references constitute the primary academic seam that binds criticism in the journal's launch period. This record suggests that the launch period was one in which perspectives were united over a very small collection of common insights.

A Struggle for Terminology: *First Person Scholar* and "Middle State" Publications

A related effort to encourage academic possibilities and field growth over discipline-specific understandings can be charted in *First Person Scholar*'s use of the phrase "middle state publication." *First Person Scholar* is an initiative of the University of Waterloo's Games Institute and "The Interactive and Multi-Modal Experience Research Syndicate" (IMMERSe). On *First Person Scholar*'s "About Us" page, the periodical concludes its self-description by stating: "First Person Scholar is a middle state publication." While the phrase is not detailed in the "About FPS" document, the declaration is immediately followed by an invitation, "If you would like to know more about that you can read any of these articles we have published on the topic and/or watch the three minute video about FPS below!" As phrased, the sentence conveys the notion that "the topic" is a subject of some interest, but what is not necessarily evident in the phrasing is the fact that "middle state publication" is a concept generated within FPS. This inference can be made not only from an extensive review of online databases, but also from the list of linked sources, which contains Emma Vossen's "Publish or Perish: Or Publish with Purpose" (2016b), Steve Wilcox's "On the Publishing Methods of Our Time: Mobilizing Knowledge in Game Studies" (2015), Jason Hawreliak's "Hybrid Publishing: The Case for the Middle State" (2013), Bart Simon's "Difficult Writing" (2016), Emma Vossen's "Academic Vigilantism" (2016a), and a YouTube video featuring Emma Vossen entitled "First Person Scholar: Publish with Purpose" (2016).

The ordering of the list is relevant to readers' emerging understandings of "middle state publication." The items are not listed in either alphabetical order or chronological order, though it is true that Vossen's opening "Publish or Perish" (2016b) is the companion to the list's concluding entry, the video "First Person Scholar: Publish with Purpose" (2016). In that opening entry, Vossen provided a link to a piece to Steve Wilcox's 2013 "Feed-Forward Scholarship: Why Game Studies Needs Middle State Publishing." There, Wilcox presents the term as his own and defines it as follows:

> Middle-state publishing refers to publications that persist between informal, decentralized blog posts, and formal, centralized journal articles. Middle-state publications typically accept submissions from a wide audience, they publish frequently, and address emergent issues in a timely fashion. In short, they are digital publications that have the timeliness of blogs but the critical attention to detail of a journal.

Vossen echoes much of this language in "Publish or Perish." For example, she describes "middle state publication" as a "website that publishes middle state writing" and then describes "middle state writing" as writing "that is somewhere between the poles of quick digital published writing like blogging and academic writing."

However, a slightly different view of "middle state publication" and "middle state writing" emerges in the next listed item, which is a journal article by Wilcox published in October 2015 in *Scholarly and Research Communication.* In it, Wilcox defines the middle state as writing "in development, with the intent of soliciting feedback at a time when ideas are just beginning to take shape." The phrasing is distinct from Vossen's description of middle state publication and middle state writing with respect to notions of completeness and academic quality, and also academic community, and is perhaps the first notion in the listing that "middle state publication" has unsettled meaning(s). This sense can also be inferred in the third item on the list, Jason Hawreliak's "Hybrid Publishing: The Case for the Middle State" (2013). Initially, Hawreliak describes "middle state publishing" in ways that are keeping with Wilcox; in 2013, he notes that middle state publishing offers "the timeliness and succinctness of a blog, while retaining the rigor and context of a conventional journal article." However, he then takes the term "middle state" and begins to use it in inscrutable ways. For example, he starts to talk about the game *State of Decay* as an ideal "middle state game" because of its low price point and mid-range production values. As used here, "middle state" seems to be laden with notions of financial accessibility and middling quality—a sense not expressed by Vossen but which is arguably inherent in Wilcox's characterization of middle state writing as "writing in development" in 2015.

The two remaining editorials in the FPS listing do not help to clarify these definition issues, but do associate the phrase with acts of supposed virtuous intellectual resistance. Writing in 2016, Bart Simon claims that "middle state publishing exists because traditional academic writing is an oppressive force that keeps our knowledge locked up in the light of academic libraries and keeps those not privileged enough to be part of the academy in the dark." Vossen, also, in 2016, goes on to use this same phrasing in her call-to-arms YouTube video. Simon's claim, which I'm offering as a representative sample from the piece, appears to be mostly groundless in terms of its sourcing, though it is true that Simon references Vossen in his assertions, and on this subject Vossen elsewhere references a specific article by Brendan Keogh, "Across Worlds and Bodies: Criticism in the Age of Video Games." Hawreliak too makes an aside to an interview with Keogh in his piece, and in such a way as to suggest that Keogh's commentary has compelled him to consider and advocate for "middle state publishing." Finally, the list of prose pieces concludes again with Vossen, who by 2016 was defining the term as "a liminal publication that is both inside and outside the academy, an organized space for critique and experimentation that is both respected for doing something different, but also disrespected for the same reason." That is to say, by 2016 "middle state publishing" appears to be laden with assumed virtues, and FPS is eager to signal them as part of its audience education process.

FPS then takes the perhaps extraordinary step of using the term to label and organize a number of other web-based publications, out of which only one self-identifies—with significant qualification—as a middle state publication: *Not Your Mama's Gamer*. We'll return to that interesting—and perhaps telling—exception in a moment. For now, it is enough to note that the rest of the list includes *Game Studies 101*, *Critical Distance*, and *Memory Insufficient*. In its act of labeling these so-called middle state publications, FPS is asserting that its term has critical values for understanding these sites and their contents. This is a motion toward field formatting, to use Juul's phrasing.

FPS' efforts to establish and present "middle state" to the reader exist in a larger rhetorical context, one that speaks to the how it is the publication frames and launches the phrase for consideration. That context itself is fascinating, as it too speaks to the site's larger efforts to move "open" and accessible conversations on games into academic and discipline-specific discourses on games and gaming cultures. I'll show how this happens with, again, concepts borrowed from Philip E. Smith's work on mission statements in Higher Education.

Smith's scheme can be used to make the following observations about FPS' "About FPS" description, which is delivered in four short segments. With emphasis added, the first segment reads:

> We at FPS are advocating for a new dynamic, one in which we demonstrate our relevancy through timely, rigorous, and accessible criticism that challenges all players to engage in what Mary Flanagan calls *critical play*.

In terms of Smith's scheme, the passage can generally be associated with public rhetoric—with the notable exceptions of "accessible criticism" and the reference to Many Flanagan's concept of "critical play." "Accessible criticism" might be associated with the rhetoric of academic inquiry, while Flanagan's "critical play" might be associated with disciplinary insiders associated with game studies. So in this opening passage, we see a blending of Smith's three modes, with a priority placed on public rhetoric that moves to and through the rhetoric of academic insiders to arrive at a discipline-specific term.

In its next portion, the statement offers more that can be associated with the rhetoric of academic inquiry. Portion two reads:

> The articles we publish encourage players—be they developers, scholars, critics, or enthusiasts—to consider alternatives to popular interpretations of games, game play, and games culture. Through this discourse we seek to establish and sustain a critical conversation amongst those producing and playing games, demonstrating in the process that the player is a figure capable of enriching and challenging our understanding of games and what they are capable of.

References to articles, discourse, and critical conversations move the passage into the rhetoric of academic inquiry, as it might be understood by interdisciplinary bodies. Notably, at least in the context of passage one, passage two does not deploy terminology that speaks to disciplinary insiders, at least not with discipline-specific phrasing. However, it is true that the values and goals expressed in this second portion are certainly in keeping with those expressed by Flanagan in her book *Critical Play: Radical Game Design*. It would be an overstatement to argue that the language is a mere distillation of Flanagan's discipline-specific prose into a more general language of academic inquiry. But the language's compatibility with Flanagan's sentiments affirms the association with Flanagan in portion one for a certain audience and is understandable as academic in nature to an even broader audience. Thus, one observation that can be made here is that the writing extends Flanagan's concerns to an audience invested in traditional notions of academic inquiry. This effort becomes particularly important by the end of the "About FPS" statement, when "middle state publication" first emerges, as it is followed by rhetorical structures that seem to have the same basic purpose.

However, prior to that, in its third portion, the passage takes a hard turn back toward public rhetoric:

> We are looking for unique and diverse perspectives that may be underrepresented in games writing, as well as those that exist between the more industry-driven journalistic view and the more traditional academic position. This means that we are especially interested in submissions from people of color, queer folks, women, and non-binary individuals.

Key concepts like "unique and diverse perspectives," "industry-driven journalist view," and the listing of various people do not require an understanding of the rhetoric of academic insiders to comprehend or appreciate. Arguably, "traditional academic position" could be associated with the rhetoric of academic insiders, but overall the language here is an effort to be comprehended by a so-called public readership. The move is noteworthy, particularly in light of the second portion, as it indicates a return to, and significant investment in, public discourse.

Finally, in its closing passage, FPS introduces the term "middle state publication" and indicates that the term is relevant to academic insiders and disciplinary insiders by associating it with game studies-centric publications and FPS articles, which are literally a mix of blog editorials and academic commentary. This work, like the paragraph following the Flanagan reference, is designed to inform the reader on the critical term, though here the effort is explicit instead of implicit. The reasoning for this shift is, of course, quite obvious, "middle state publication" is essentially an in-house term for FPS, and demands clarification for all kinds of readerships, public, academic, and disciplinary.

Smith's scheme can be used to characterize the FPS "About Us" statement as a statement bookend with discipline-specific terms, one external to the publication and one internal to the publication. These terms are linked by an interplay of public rhetoric and the rhetoric of academic insiders. In its opening moves, the statement works to inform the reader on the concept of critical play, and in its conclusion the statement promises to inform the reader on the concept of middle state publication. The structural repetition can lead to the observation that both terms have discipline-specific relevance beyond the "About FPS" statement. Whether or not they do is perhaps a debatable point. Perhaps the best evidence of this can be inferred from the way *Not Your Mama's Gamer* (NYMG) chose to deploy the term in its own mission statement in 2015. There, NYMG claims to be not a "middle state publication," but instead a "peer-reviewed middle state publication." The need for the qualifying phrase "peer-reviewed" seems noteworthy, to the extent that it conveys a sense of unease with respect to where, exactly, it is between the poles of blogging and rigorous academic scholarship that "middle state publication" may be located by those in the know.

Game Studies: The International Journal of Computer Games Research and *First Person Scholar* present discipline-specific efforts to expand access to game studies scholarship—and to promote such scholarship, of course. These efforts contribute to an atmosphere of intellectual inclusion that begins with generalist associations between fields, the kinds that normalize and facilitate the sorts of conversations on poverty that have emerged in relevant scholarship to date. Certainly, it is not my intention to indicate that these publications are descriptive of the field as a whole, but their extended relevance to the field—and in particular to the 2010s—makes them relevant to the investigation at hand and, to the general, public-facing conceptions of poverty in works included in Gray and Leonard's *Woke Gaming: Digital Challenges to Oppression and Social Injustice*. For example, to the extent that such "field formatting" efforts prioritize interdisciplinarity over discipline-specific understanding, and to the extent that they prioritize public-facing discussions of interdisciplinary subjects, it is not surprising that even as late as the 2010s terms like "economics" and "poverty" are incorporated into associated monographs without extensive qualifications or specifications. To the extent that *Game Studies* and *First Person Scholar* can be associated with Juul's "gold rush" and its continuing legacy, these publications can stand as rationales for the field's ongoing and (importantly) meaningful engagement with general concepts aimed at academic audiences. A challenge, then, for the project at hand—with its special focus on poverty as theme—is to move out from such concepts into critical fields that are poised to present discipline-specific conceptions of poverty thematics relevant to the discipline-expanding questions about identity that have come to define game studies as a field in the first, second, and now third decades of the twenty-first century.

A Struggle for Recognition: *Not Your Mama's Gamer*'s Transition from Blog to Journal

A sense of just how challenging it can be to generate, sustain, and promote such movement can be ascertained from a consideration of the public-facing blog *Not Your Mama's Gamer*'s (NYMG) efforts to associate the site with an academic journal. This work can begin with a consideration of both the blog and journal's citation record. By "citation record," I mean the record of academic works that cite these publications and also the record for such works that have themselves been cited in other, traditional academic documents: for example, theses, journal articles, chapters in edited collections, and monographs.[18] To the extent that this effort illuminates the challenges scholars moving into game studies from extra-academic or academic fields not yet associated with game studies face, it reveals what may be at stake for traditional notions of academic discourse in current game studies-centric scholarship.

The *NYMG* Journal has developed out of the *NYMG* Blog, which was launched in 2011 by Samantha Blackmon and Alex Layne. On the blog's "about" page, Blackmon and Layne explain that the blog "was designed as a space that would bring scholarly endeavors in line with personal passion, a space that would combine feminist interrogation of games with the games community."[19] The blog's focus, they explain, "has always been … the unpacking of games from a feminist perspective, and having a good time while we're at it." They then note that, in 2015, they "began planning a careful shift to a peer-reviewed middle-state publication offering a dedicated space to feminist game studies." The first issue of that publication appeared in April 2018, and a second issue appeared in December 2019.

The April 2018 issue contains four items, a "Letter from the Editor" authored by Blackman and then two articles: Lauren Woolbright and Marie Jarrell's "Framing *The Blood of the Vampire*: A Text-Based Game" and Elizabeth Ballou's "Where *The Witcher 3: The Wild Hunt* Goes Wrong in Depicting Women (and Why It Matters)." The issue also contains a video adaptation and associated transcript of a keynote delivered by Adrianne Shaw at the 2017 *Critical Game Studies Symposium* at University of California Irvine titled "Are We There Yet?: The Politics and Practice of Intersectional Feminist Game Studies." As of this writing, only Shaw's piece has been cited. It has been cited in four texts: Bonnie Ruberg and Amanda Philips' "Not Gay as in Happy: Queer Resistance in Video Games," from the December 2018 issue of *Game Studies* (cited itself twenty times); Amanda Philips' monograph *Gamer Trouble* (2020, cited itself fourteen times); another article also by Philips titled "Negg(at)ing the Game Studies Subject: An Affective History of the Field" (cited five times) published in the Winter 2020 edition of *Feminist Media Studies;* and Alisha Karabinus' "Games and Technical Communication at the Crossroads: Defining and Designing Game Studies" (2019, cited zero times from the proceedings of the 37th Association for Computing Machinery's International Conference on the Design of Communication).

With respect to the *NYMG* Journal Issue one, then, we can observe that the document published a single work, Shaw's, that has moved out into the field with some noteworthy success. I will review a scheme for commenting on that apparent success momentarily. First, however, let's consider the citation record for the *NYMG* Journal's second issue. In terms of the second issue, the following observations can be made. It contains three pieces: "A Letter from the Editor" again by Blackmon, and two essays: Anna Burns' "A Case Study of Transgender Representation in Video Games: *Mass Effect*'s Hainly Abrams" and Jamie L. McDaniel's "Accessibility and Ableism in Tabletop Business Games." As of this writing, neither piece has a record of citation on Google Scholar or through Academic Search Premier Databases.

The question of why a limited but noteworthy citation record can be sourced to the journal's first volume but not to its second volume might lead to considerations of simple timing—as more than three years have passed since the publication of the first issue and not yet two years have passed since the publication of the second issue. Similar reasoning might consider the likely impact of a pandemic on academic production during the entirety of the span that has passed since the publication of issue two. One might also consider the possibility that Shaw simply has the most productive citation record in the *NYMG* Journal roster (some 1300 citations): Blackmon (273), Woolbright (42), Jarrell (21), Burns (~5), and McDaniel (6). However, these considerations are only assumptions. For this reason, it may be useful to ask how the *NYMG* Journal citation record might be considered in the citation record for the larger NYMG Blog, and if the journal citation record is indicative of a larger publication-specific trend.

The initial cited reference to the blog appears in 2013, in Issue No 2 of *Ada: A Journal of Gender, New Media, and Technology.* Layne and Blackmon's "Self-Saving Princess: Feminism and Post-play Narrative Modding" is included in that issue, and the piece makes reference to *nymgamer.com*. The essay itself has gone on to be cited some eighteen times since 2013. That figure is roughly equivalent to the number of times Ruberg and Philips' "Not Gay as in Happy: Queer Resistance in Video Games" (twenty times) has been cited. The difference is that nearly a decade has passed since *Self-Saving Princess* was published and only three years since the *NYMG* Journal item associated with Ruberg and Philips' work was published. Also in 2013, Sarah Nixon's "Applying the Bechdel Test to Video Games" was published in *NYMG*. It now carried three citations, starting in 2016.

No citations were made to *NYMG* items in 2014 or 2015 (or, to date, to works published during that period on the blog). As a side note, I find this interesting as Blackmon and Layne indicate elsewhere that this is the same period during which they began to think about expanding their blogging efforts with an academic journal—this may have been a period of developing aspirations for the site. However, while that journal work was developing, the blog started to pick up more citations: indeed more than the journal has yet to receive. For example, in 2016 there are three cited references to *NYMGamer*, but only one of them has itself been cited since. The piece, from the proceedings of the first international joint conference of DiGRA and Foundation of Digital Games (FDG) is Cosima Rughinis, Razvan Rughinis, and Elisabeta Toma's "Three Shadowed Dimensions of Feminine Presence in Video Games," and it cited the aforementioned piece by Sarah Nixon: "Applying the Bechdel Test to Video Games."

In 2017, there is some limited movement: there are six cited references, but of those two of the six have gone on to themselves be cited. The first is a PhD thesis by Iain James Timothy Hart titled "Ludomusicological Semiotics: Theory, Implications, and Case Studies," which cites a piece by Ian Bogost, "Epistemological Gatekeeping, and the Holodeck" from a May 2017 publication on *NYMGamer*. Hart's dissertation has since been cited in two other works. The other item in an edited connection on Writing Studies programs has gone on to be cited a number of times, thirty-three times so far, but these subsequent citations cannot be attributed to the document's engagement with *NYMG* or Games Studies-related content, generally.

The year 2018 marks a year of noteworthy growth for the blog. There are eleven cited references to NYMG, and of those eleven, six have gone on to be cited elsewhere. Of the articles that have been cited elsewhere, the number of citations range from one to thirty-three. The two most widely cited items, in order of citation, are Linda K. Kaye, Charlotte

R. Pennington, and Joseph J. McCann's "Do Casual Gaming Environments Evoke Stereotype Threat? Examining the Effects of Explicit Priming and Avatar Gender" (thirty-three citations) from the collection *Computers and Human Behavior*, and Jason Hawreliak's monograph *Multimodal Semiotics and Rhetoric in Videogames* (sixteen citations).

The year 2019 marked a year of advancing growth for the blog. There are twenty-two citations, and of those nine have been cited elsewhere. As we get closer to the present, we, of course, must allow for the fact that there has simply been less time for the works that are engaged with *NYMG* to be picked up by other works. Of those nine items, only three have more than about one or two associated citations: one item is cited three times, another four times, but then there is a contextually remarkable association with Clara Fernandez-Vara's *Introduction to Game Analysis*, which has been cited 237 times. Vara references a blog post by Blackmon "Pickaninnies and Pixels: On Race, Racism, and Cuphead at E3," from 2015. Of 2020 and 2021, the following observations can be made—and again here we need to allow for the lack of a significant interval since the time of original publication, and also for the pandemic: in 2020 there are fifteen citations, yielding six subsequently cited works, and in 2021 there have been three, yielding, not surprisingly, no subsequently cited works to date.

A review of the *NYMGamer Blog* suggests that, at present, the blog is cited more frequently by academic works than its associated journal. This raises questions of whether or not the blog's investment in a journal structure may represent an academic bias on the part of the editors that is essentially invalidated by the blog's acceptance in the broader academic community already, as represented not only with citations but by the involved works that have themselves gone on to be cited subsequently in other corners of the academy. One implication of these findings is that the concept of "journal" may not be particularly significant to *NYMGamer*'s presence in the field. Given that game studies as a discipline can be associated with a number of works that prioritize interdisciplinary associations, as is the case with *GameStudies.org Game Studies: The International Jorunal of Computer Games Research* and *First Person Scholar*, it is perhaps not at all unexpected that *NYMG*'s general blog would generate a more robust citation record than would that blog's associated academic journal.

These observations present one view—a select view—of the field in development, at least at the level of electronic, academic periodicals. These details suggest a field that is moving quickly across various levels of the academy, but it does not yet suggest a field that has coalesced around an internalized set of discipline-specific concepts, or at least not in a way that would extend from common citation practices that could be linked back to a short list of academic works with extended relevance to the field. This view of game-studies-in-development underscores what is "at stake" when one is discussing videogame poverty themes. For example, are such concepts urgent for understanding the conventions of play, the implications of play, or even the economic perspectives of the player or the played? To the extent that this book makes use of the transmedia concept of slumming to frame considerations of poverty thematics, it participates in the academic tradition characterized in this chapter—that is, it reaches beyond the field to locate and deploy context(s) for analysis. To the extent that such efforts might illuminate the subject at hand—that is, representations of poverty in videogames—it constitutes a view of games and gaming that stands to be tried and possibly refined under future considerations. However, such work, like all of the work that stands to be considered, reconsidered, and expanded upon in the journals reviewed in this chapter, depends on an essential assumption: namely, that the relevant insights are meaningful beyond the scope of their associated arguments' interpretive scheme or schemes.

Notes

1. Kocurek, 121.
2. Juul, *Half-Real*, Introduction.
3. Castronova, *Exodus*, Chapter 3.
4. Dyer-Witheford, *Games*, 225.
5. Ibid., 105.
6. Snodgrass, 139.
7. Pearce, "Exploring."
8. Martoncik, "Do."
9. Welsh, 112.
10. Ibid., 360.
11. Galloway, "Social Realism."
12. Jayemanne, *Performativity*, 2.
13. Ibid., 173.
14. GameStudies.org
15. Aarseth, http://www.gamestudies.org/0101/editorial.html
16. Aarseth, http://gamestudies.org/2101/articles/aarseth_anniversary
17. Smith, 34.
18. To locate this record, I have consulted and cross-referenced Google Scholar and EBSCO holdings. I singled these resources out on the basis of their accessibility in the United States Public Library systems (rather than

on the basis of their comprehensiveness). As game studies is a discipline that, to borrow a word from Murray, often "teeters" between academic and non-academic audiences, the Google Scholar and EBSCO databases felt particularly appropriate as they are ready resources for both communities. So, the overall caveat for what follows is that I am not arguing for an objective citation record, but rather for a citation record as it is represented in these select databases.

19. NMGamer.com/About

Bibliography

Aarseth, Espen. *Cybertext: Perspectives on Ergodic Literature.* Baltimore: John Hopkins University Press, 1997.

Castronova, Edward. *Exodus to the Virtual World: How Online Fun is Changing Reality.* Palgrave Macmillan, 2007. Kindle edition.

Geraci, Robert M. *Virtually Sacred: Myth and Meaning in* World of Warcraft *and* Second Life. New York: Oxford University Press, 2014. Kindle edition.

Hertz, J.C. *Joystick Nation: How Videogames Gobbled Our Money, Won Our Hearts and Rewired our Minds.* Little, Brown and Company 1997.

Hawreliak, Jason. "Hybrid Publishing: The Case for the Middle State." *First Person Scholar*, 2013. http://www.firstpersonscholar.com/the-case-for-the-middle-state/.

Hayden, Craig. "The Procedural Rhetorics of Mass Effect: Video Games as Argumentation in International Relations." *International Studies Perspectives* (2017): 175–193.

Jayemanne, Darshana. *Performativity in Art, Literature, and Videogames.* Palgrave Macmillan, 2017. Kindle edition.

Krobová, T., Moravec, O., & Švelch, J. (2015). Dressing Commander Shepard in pink: Queer playing in a heteronormative game culture. *Cyberpsychology: Journal of Psychosocial Research on Cyberspace, 9*(3), Article 3. https://doi.org/10.5817/CP2015-3-3.

Mukherjee, Souvik. *Video Games and Storytelling: Reading Games and Playing Books.* Palgrave Macmillan, 2015. Kindle edition.

Murray, Janet H. *Hamlet on the Holodeck: The Future of Narrative in Cyberspace.* Free Press, 1997. Kindle edition.

Pearce, Alyssa Maria. "Exploring Performance of Gendered Identities through Language in *World of Warcraft.*" *International Journal of Human–Computer Interaction*, 33:3, (2017) 180–189, https://doi.org/10.1080/10447318.2016.1230965.

Simon, Bart. "Difficult Writing." First Person Scholar (2016). http://www.firstpersonscholar.com/difficult-writing/

Smith, Philip E. "The Mission of Rhetoric and the Rhetoric of Mission Statements." ADE Bulletin, no 121. (Winter 1998): 30–36.
Snodgrass, Jeffrey G. "Online virtual worlds as anthropological field sites: Ethnographic methods training via collaborative research of Internet gaming cultures." *Annals of Anthological Practice* 40, no. 2 (November 2016): 134–147.
Stark, David K. "Grand Theft Architecture: Architectural Works in Video Games after E.S.S. Entertainment v. Rockstar Games," Berkeley Technology Law Journal 25, no. 1 (2010): 429–464.
Vossen, Emma "Academic Vigilantism." *First Person Scholar*, 2016a. http://www.firstpersonscholar.com/academic-vigilantism-and-middle-state-publishing/
Vossen, Emma "Academic Vigilantism." First Person Scholar. "Publish or Perish: Or Publish with Purpose." *First Person Scholar* (2016b). http://www.firstpersonscholar.com/publish-or-perish/.
Welsh, Timothy J. *Mixed Realism: Videogames and the Violence of Fiction*. Minneapolis: University of Minnesota Press, 2017. Kindle edition.
Wilcox, Steve. "On the Publishing Methods of Our Time: Mobilizing Knowledge in Game Studies" *Scholarly and Research Communication 6,* issue 3, (2015)

CHAPTER 5

Human Subjects and Digital Poverty

Game Studies: The Player and The Played

The possibility that poverty might have a thematic expression in one or some collection of videogames raises questions of whether or not the videogame form might limit or somehow shape such expressions. As already discussed, the videogame form has been usefully associated with notions of interactivity, but the always-developing nature of new media underscores the notion that formalist assertions may be short-lived. Of course, though some aspect of the videogame form might be transitory, that does not mean that it could not be significant to a thematic expression of one sort or another. The relevance of the videogame form to a thematic expression—of poverty or some other subject—is not diminished by a form's diminishing relevance to conceptions of videogames over time. Analysis, then, might begin with a question of how form and theme might be associated, when and where they can be. A review of noteworthy contributions to game studies over the past decade illustrates and models how such analysis might be rationalized and deployed. It also establishes a context for how the concept of videogame poverty thematics might be productively associated with several academic disciplines beyond game studies.

Established work that lays a foundation for such efforts can be located, for example, in the writing of Frédérik Lesage. Lesage considers Igor Kopytoff's concept of "cultural biographies" to consider digital media and

A. Crowley, *Representations of Poverty in Videogames*, https://doi.org/10.1007/978-3-031-00144-4_5

proceeds under the premise that "Biographies of things enable the researcher to trace the tension between a thing's classification within abstracted ideal cultural categories such as commodity and how a specific instance of a thing is reclassified through its real-life existence."[1] With respect to the argument at hand, the concept of cultural biography is a concept in-kind with the notion of the player's act of play, to the extent that the intersection of player and game substantiates, at least in part, a game's "real-life existence." As the concept of "real-life existence" is quite non-specific, Lesage finds it useful later in his argument to turn to the work of Jussi Parikka, who offers the term "cultural condensation points" to identify intersections of "materials, cultural forms, practices and discourse of subjectification."[2] Lesage turns to this notion at the exact moment in his argument that he takes on the concept of "media software," and he argues that the concept can be used to undergird a new "media archeology," one that would provide "a historical methodology to frame the media-thing by tracing its topological arrangement through media discourses and diagrams." The promise of such work, he argues, can be found in "its skepticism toward linear histories and dominant narratives"[3] and its related capacity for "opening up a new approach to situating biographical account of digital things like media software."

Related work that shows the promise of such thinking can be found in scholarship offered by Stacy L. Smith, Ken Lachlan, and Ron Tamborini. In their study, "Popular Video Games: Quantifying the Presentation of Violence and Its Content," they explore "60 of the most popular video games for violence from three gaming systems"[4] and come to the useful observation that games' ratings were not only indicative of relative levels of violence within game but were also correlated with distinctive context for violence—that is, "mature games were more likely to feature child perpetrators" and "also justified acts of repeated gun violence that are graphic in nature."[5] This work leads the authors to conclude that "The basic prototype or template for aggression in teen/mature video games is a human perpetrator engaging in repeated acts of justified violence involving weapons that result in some bloodshed to the victim."[6] They note that this same template also exists in general audience games, though there "the template for violence … is that attractive nonhumans engage in violence using their own natural means." These notions lead the authors to conclude that "video games … pose risk for development of aggressive scripts for social problem solving."[7] With respect to Parikka and Lesage, the work of Smith et al. projects the boundaries of a limited study onto all cultural forms associated with the term "video game." Without dismissing their analysis of the violence templates they see in general audience and mature audience games, it is possible to ask if such templates are simply fundamental to the videogame form within market economies that cater to (or work to instill and satisfy) violent desires. Or, to put it another way, it is not entirely clear what the authors mean when they use the term "video game," though it is clear that they are using the term to encapsulate the sixty titles they identify in their study.

A related effort can be found in the work of Daniel Punday, who considers games in which the experience of loss "is understood as a form of melancholy rather than morning and trauma." In contrast to the work of Smith et al., Punday's consideration of melancholy and "transmedia morning" touches on only a few actual titles—*Lolli's Apartment*, *Grim Fandango*, and *Half-Life*—and it conveys none of the categorial certainties offered by Smith et al.[8] However, Punday's efforts to rationalize emotional commonalities across titles, and in ways that attend to similarly structured experiences of loss, lead to the useful notion that the player's act of play can intersect with a gaming template that works to script player's action and also to ensure that such actions resonate with other acts of play associated with other titles. With respect to media archology, if games are to be considered "cultural condensation points," the question emerges of whether or not the relevant intersecting "materials, cultural forms, practices and discourse of subjectification" are doomed to produce variations of one template (Smith et al.) or if, as Punday and, elsewhere, Welsh, have argued, they might produce templates that are as varied as the very factors that prefigure and condition their cultural emergence. With respect to Murray, interest in this binary should be tempered by the notion that market forces surely intervene to determine the kinds of templates that are expressed within and across cultures. To this notion, we might also add a concept that Murray herself could not have considered when she was writing in the late 1990s: namely, how has the development of game studies itself shaped the kinds of questions that we might ask about significant economic contexts bearing on the player and the played, and the intersection of these subjects? In this chapter, we will consider a humanist context for such considerations and apply it to scholarship concerned with related discourses of subjectification with relevance to the representation of the poor and impoverished in videogames.

Game Studies: Addressing the Proper Subject—Opportunities for Growth

Alexander Pope's poem "Essay on Man" (1733) is perhaps best known today for its opening lines: "Know then thyself, presume not God to scan; The proper study of Mankind is man."[9] In the context of Pope's writing, the decree reflects a deep dissatisfaction with what Stephen Greenblatt describes as a "period of rapid moral, political, and cultural deterioration" that coincided with the "reigns of George I and George II" (2667).[10] Though "Essay on Man" is nearly 300 years old, the poem and its exigency can still illuminate modern humanist inquiries, including the kind that have been so significant to the academic subfield generally known as game studies over the last half-decade.

At the level of monograph, the recent past has been a period of increased academic visibility for this subject area, due in no small part to conferences in the Popular Culture/American Culture circuit, which has fueled and also been fueled by a steady stream of publications from the University of Minnesota Press, MIT Press, Palgrave, Routledge, McFarland, and others. A review of such work reveals developing considerations of the human subjects that exist within and between gaming contexts. Without dismissing or diminishing the relevance of earlier scholarship, it can be argued that these selections stand in stark contrast to many notable, late twentieth- and early twenty-first-century monographs associated with game studies: for example, Janet H. Murray's *Hamlet on the Holodeck* (1997), Edward Castronova's *Synthetic Worlds: The Business and Culture of Online Games* (2005), Mackenzie Wark's *Gamer Theory* (2007), and Ian Bogost's *Persuasive Games: The Expressive Power of Videogames* (2010). Such titles, generally speaking, attend to abstract gaming contexts that exist in loose association with unspecified human subjects. The distinction between the early and recent works, to return to Pope, is one in which the human figure of the "gamer" has been moved into critical focus, not at the expense of broader queries into the abstractions of "gaming," but rather so that we might have a better understanding of what we are talking about when we are talking about "gaming."

The movement to and interest in the human subject has coincided with meaningful claims from critics about the kinds of audiences that can benefit from a consideration of game studies scholarship. For example, in her review of Shaw's *Gaming at the Edge*, Stephanie Orme characterizes that work as being of interest to "representation scholars."[11] Elsewhere, in her review of Kocurek's *Coin-Operated Americans*, Meredith A. Bak finds that the text will be of interest to those concerned with topics as wide ranging as "intersection among media, technology, and critical questions surrounding children and youth."[12] E. Deshane casts the assumed net of interest even wider and simply uses the pronoun "we" to indicate the possible audience for Ruberg and Shaw's *Queen Game Studies*, which, Deshane claims, charts an "imagined borderland that we can populate with new experiences, new queerness, and new games."[13] In her review of Shira Chess' *Ready Player Two*, Esther MacCallum-Stewart is less dramatic but also quite general and claims that the text will "resonate strongly in wider critical arguments about gendered play and leisure activities."[14] Finally, Kyle Millian, in his comments on Condis' *Gaming Masculinity*, claims that the text is "[f]or those who consider themselves avid gamers to those who have never picked up a video game in their life" (web).[15] This last claim is perhaps the most notable, as it literally assumes all of humanity.

Grand or not-so-grand (and accurate or not-so-accurate), the awareness these reviewers express about possible audiences for these texts is essentially absent in the initial reviews of some of the subject-area's early monographs. For example, the 1997 Kirkus review of Murray's *Hamlet on the Holodeck* makes no gesture to a possible audience for the text, though it does celebrate the effort as "exciting."[16] The same can be said of Toby Madden's review of Castronova's *Synthetic Worlds*, which does not imagine an audience for the text but does find the text to be "very satisfying."[17] Vince Carducci's review of Wark's *Gamer Theory* is similarly accepting of the text, even if it does not identify an audience that might be interested in the text.[18] It's not until 2010, in the review of Bogost's *Persuasive Games*, that the notion of audience really begins to creep in to major reviews. For example, Rudy McDaniel makes the claim that the work "is fascinating for anyone immersed in the field of literary or linguistic computing (and especially for those readers with a foothold in game studies, game design, game criticism, or even cultural studies)."[19]

Certainly, just because some of the reviewers failed to note potential audiences for Murray, Castronova, and Wark's efforts, that does not mean that audiences did not exist for those efforts. However, the frequency with which contemporary reviewers are addressing game studies monographs in terms of audience can be read as an indication that game studies is maturing as a field of study and is expanding in its relevance to other subject areas. While it is simply too early to tell if the scholarship of our moment will itself give rise to subsequent works with equal or greater appeal to humanist endeavors, it seems to me perfectly reasonable to observe that game studies is raising its profile, so to speak. While this prospect is and should be exciting for scholars seeking to take an active hand in our common transformative moment, it is important to note that the prospect of broader academic significance for game studies arrives with increased demands on game studies scholars to be aware not only of their own research but also of the relevance of that research to other, established fields.

The seriousness of the situation is conveyed quite well in lines found elsewhere in the writing of Alexander Pope. In his *Essay on Criticism* (1711), Pope addresses those who would "justly bear a critic's noble name." Pope admonishes would-be critics to "Be sure your self and your own reach to know,/ How far your genius, taste, and learning go;/ Launch not beyond your depth, but be discreet, /And mark the point where sense and dulness meet."[20] For Pope, the danger for scholars who fail to heed this warning is dire, as "a fool in verse makes many more in prose." While the concept of "fool" is a harsh one, the significance of Pope's point to game studies can be illuminated with a consideration of some of field's early rhetorical tropes: for example, Murray and Castronova conclude their efforts with what I'll call the "Nostradamus turn" and dole out heavy-handed yet noticeably non-specific predictions about the future significance of their chosen subjects of study to the wider world. For example, Murray writes, "Looking ahead to the next forty years – the working life of the generation that has grown up with videogames and educational computing tools – we can expect a range of narrative formats to emerge as authors look for ways to preserve the customary pleasures of linear narrative while exploiting the essential properties of the digital medium with increasing sophistication."[21] From Castronova, "Early visionaries saw a single 'metaverse' that is said to exist in parallel with our universe; but we can already see that the synthetic world will resolve itself into a thousand islands, each separated from the next by many miles of ocean."[22] As is always the case, such predictive and assumptive language can be arrested at the moment of its composition with a simple question: why?

Second to the "Nostradamus turn" is the equally estranging move let's call the "navel ascension," in which the critic asserts the significance of his or her subject area by turning away from the rest of the word with astonishing speed—and vanishing. For example, from Wark, "From this vantage point, the whole of cultural history can be rethought. It is not a question of adding games as the tail end of a history of forms but of rethinking the whole of cultural history after the digital game."[23] Without resorting to the sometimes tortured reasoning that these and other authors have since offered in support of such claims, the basic desire to hypothesize future academic relevance without evidence may invite interest but it absolutely courts incredulity.

Pope's warning, however, is more profound than a simple admonishment against speaking about things you do not and cannot understand. The instruction to "be discreet" while attending to the limits of sense, but not beyond, carries with it an awareness of the complexities involved in generating human knowledge, which come not only from the challenges of intellectual pursuit but also from the revolutionary nature of scholarship itself, which stands to undo the scholar's surety in self and in that which is supposedly "known." One of the unifying features of the recent game studies monographs addressed in this text is an explicit or implicit awareness of this challenge. For the purposes of brevity, I'll again use Carly A. Kocurek's *Coin-Operated Americans* as a representative example. The author considers "the development of the 'video gamer' as a cultural identity during video gaming's first decade."[24] In her exploration, Kocurek works diligently and productively to establish an economic context for the 1970s that is specific to the emergence of her chosen subject. The author pulls from a range of reasonable sources to accomplish this task: for example, from the Bureau of Labor Statistics, as well as from cultural theorists such as David Harvey and Fredric Jameson. What emerges from the work is a compelling argument on the significance of a series of economic "upheavals" that collectively shaped cultural conditions that, the author contends, made it possible for the "video gamer" to materialize into our common understanding of twentieth-century identities.

With respect to the context of a growing field, the success of Kocurek's argument—that is, to "justly bear a critic's noble name"—can be understood on two fronts: first, in the context of the argument itself, which reaches out in productive ways to and across disciplines and, second, in the broader context of an argument with shared interests, Michael Z. Neuman's *Atari Age: The Emergence of Video Games in America* (2017). Neuman's stated task in that text is to offer a "new media history of video games, charting their emergence in the United States during their first decade of public, commercial availability, beginning around 1972."[25] Without detracting from or intending to diminish in any way Newman's successful offering, it can be noted that Neuman's "new media history" is dissimilar from Kocurek's "excavation" in terms of how it is the author attempts to frame and explore significant economic issues bearing on his subject of study. Rather than use government statistics in conjunction with post-modern theories, Neuman provides extended reflections on period-specific advertisements, evaluated under postulations from Frankfurt School and Frankfurt School-related commentators.

Kocurek's and Neuman's distinct tracks for addressing economic issues that are relevant to early videogames and gamers establish a set of positions that are specific enough to compare and contrast from the perspective of either game studies or economics. For example, at the level of monograph, Kocurek's argument is perhaps most similar to Randy Nichols' *The Video Game Industry* (2014), which presents a detailed consideration of market-matters derived, in part, from corporate reports and financial data and in that effort is itself following in the steps of an even earlier work, Nick Dyer-Witheford and Greig de Peuter's *Games of Empire: Global Capitalism and Video Games* (2009). That text comes with the famously grand thesis that "video games are a paradigmatic media of Empire—planetary, militarized hypercapitalism—and of some of the forces presently challenging it." As an argument, that text establishes and explores economic realities with a mix of government and corporate reporting summoned to account under various Marxist theories. As such, the document has telltale features that, at least in terms of its efforts to establish and pursue economic issues, resonate through the works of Nichols, Newman, and Kocurek.

These texts now form a constellation of efforts that might be considered for their common or unique relationships with notions of economics and "the economy." It is also true that individually as well as collectively they stand ready for perhaps an even greater test, one that may be a good indication of whether or not such monographs (and perhaps game studies itself) will have an extended life in the marketplace of ideas. Such testing will involve a rhetorical awareness of recent, transformative contributions to the field of Economics that raise fundamental questions about the broader significance of the very markets that first gave rise to "videogames" and the "video gamer." One such contribution is Thomas Piketty's *Capital in the Twenty-First Century* (2014). The text has been lauded in *The Guardian* as a "VIB – Very Important Book,"[26] and one that will, according to *The Economist*, "influence the ways thousands of readers and plenty of economists think about wealth and income inequality."[27] Piketty takes nothing less than the global evolution of the distribution of wealth as his subject of inquiry and supports a thesis that "[a]n apparently small gap between the return on capital and the rate of growth can in the long run have powerful and destabilizing effects on the structure and dynamics of social inequality."[28] Piketty's impact has come not from his thesis necessarily, but from the success with which he marshals the first fruits of "big data" to demonstrate with remarkable clarity to people hailing from any number of backgrounds how income and wealth inequality have developed across and between nations over the last three or so centuries.

Piketty's modeling can lead to the conclusion that the 1970s, for all (and perhaps because) of its "upheavals," was a remarkably unremarkable decade, at least when it is viewed from the perspective of income and wealth inequality. Certainly, this data compels questions about why, with respect to the 1950s, 1960s, 1980s, and 1990s, the 1970s experienced essential stability for these rates within the United States.[29] In the context of Kocurek's argument, Pickett's data enables scholars to ask to what extent did the stabilization of class structures in the United States during the 1970s facilitate the "cultural identity" of the video gamer in gaming's first decade?

Additionally, his data stands ready to illuminate Kocurek's fundamental suppositions about the US economy in the 1970s, which are derived from David Harvey's *The Conditions of Postmodernity: An Enquiry into the Origins of Cultural Change* (1991). There, Harvey notes that, by the 1970s, there had been a "mobilization of fashion in mass markets [which] provided a means to accelerate the pace of consumption not only in clothing, ornament, and decoration but also across a wide swath of life-styles and recreational activities (leisure and sporting habits, music styles, video and children's games, and the like)." Harvey's second notion as reported by Kocurek is that the same period experienced a "shift away from the consumption of goods and into the consumption of services not only personal, business, educational, and health services, but also entertainments, spectacles, happenings and distractions."[30] Importantly, those claims are offered in the context of Harvey's own economic analysis, which characterizes the 1970s, in comparison to the work of Piketty, as a period of remarkable economic instability, in terms of the decade's rates of wealth and income inequality. One path then, for future contributions to the field of game studies, is to consider the question of how critics might justly "bear" that noble name by reconciling the field's past presumptions about economics with the data-driven observations the field of economics has offered recently to clarify the view of "gaming's first decade."

Game Studies' Postmodern Economics: The Avant-Pop Rides Again

Select, recent *Game Studies* publications promise and often deliver remarkably granular considerations of videogames, gamers, and gaming that promise novel insights into the relevance of poverty to the player's acts of play. Works as varied as Amy Green's *Posttraumatic Stress Disorder, Trauma, and History in Metal Gear Solid* Five (2017), Marc A. Ouellette and Jason C. Thompson's *The Post 9/11 Video Game: A Critical Examination* (2017), and Shira Chess' *Ready Player Two: Women Gamers and Designed Identity* (2017) contribute to an ever-growing body of work that's expanding how, why, and even when we talk about (and think about) games. One notable feature of this critical surge is an interest in postmodern thought, if not postmodernity itself, as evident in titles by Carly A. Kocurek (2015) and Timothy J. Welsh (2016). Such interest is exciting not only because it promises a return to (if not a revival of) postmodern analysis, but also because it charts a path for engaging class-conscious, interdisciplinary intellectual movements that have (with debatable success) arisen in defense of or in defiance to postmodern thinking. The field's ease/unease with postmodern thought might be productively associated with the Avant-Pop, for the purpose of generating interdisciplinary contexts for specifying subjects like poverty thematics.

Larry McCaffery famously launches the term "Avant-Pop" in two anthologies, *Avant-Pop: Fiction for a Daydream Nation* (1992) and *After Yesterday's Crash: The Avant-Pop Anthology* (1995). In a 1994 interview with Alexander Laurence and Jill Jacques, McCaffery explains the origins of the movement, citing his encounter with Lester Bowie and the Chicago Arts Ensemble's album, *Avant-Pop*. After listening to the first song on the record, a cover of Fats Domino's "Blueberry Hill," McCaffery noted that Bowie's "weird twisted version" was "opening [the song] up to what was already there but just needed to be let out."[31] McCaffery concluded that the effort was similar to what Kathy Acker was doing by rewriting *Great Expectations* and also what she and others like Mark Leyner were struggling with: the problem "American avant-garde artists face, and that is, how do you compete with a media that is instantly able to appropriate radical aspects of your work and put it into a Nike ad?"[32] The significance of such appropriation as it relates to videogames is hinted at in Leyner's novel, *Gone with the Mind* (2016), in which the videogame form is repeatedly referenced as the prime commercial entertainment of our common period, and Leyner raises a number of concerns about how his own life might be properly appropriated or misappropriated into a first-person shooter.

While the Avant-Pop movement has never been particularly well-defined, in 1992, Mark Amerika illuminated the Avant-Pop as it had "emerged" under postmodernism in his notorious "Avant-Pop Manifesto: Thread Baring Itself in Ten Quick Posts." In short, the posts identify Avant-Pop as a new turn in the culture that has arisen after the apparent death of the postmodern. According to Amerika, this movement is created by the "Children of Mass Media" who accept the notion that a popular culture sensibility influences how imaginations process experience.[33] These "children" are dedicated to artistic efforts that will allow them to attract "attention with the popularized forms of representation that fill up 'the contemporary Mediascape.'" To that end, they welcome the "Electronic age" with open arms and will shamelessly "sample anything they need" to address two key questions: "who are we sharing the cultural toilet with, and what are we filling it up with?"

In his document's seventh, and perhaps most notable, post, Amerika argues that the Avant-Pop does not "give a shit about your phoney social reality" as it pertains to narrative structure, claiming that fairytale structuring—for example, "Once upon a time-ing"—"doesn't interest us … .We prefer to lose ourselves in the exquisite realms of spacy sex and timeless narrative disaster … so that you no longer have to feel chained to the bed of commercial standardization."[34] For Amerika, the infrastructure by which such "exquisite realms" and "sexy space" will be delivered to "the emerging youth culture" is "the Data Superhighway" which will "finally once and for all do "away with the high-priced middlemen, and artists will reap the benefits of their own hard-earned labor."

While the concerns in Amerika's infamous ten posts persist into the present period, it is important to note that the Avant-Pop movement—if it was ever really a movement—can essentially be dated to a series of publications that, for all intents and purposes, are confined to the mid-1990s, and that its era was capped with the unexpected and untimely death of Kathy Acker from breast cancer in 1997. But the movement's essential questions for artists—for example, who are we sharing the cultural toilet with, and what are we filling it up with?—remain as valid in the present period as they did in the mid-1990s, and in the context of the movement's promised Data Superhighway with its transference of "exquisite sexy realms and timeless narrative disaster," such questions are of special value for game studies. This is underscored in three recent and previously discussed publications, Carly A. Kocurek (2015) Michael Z. Neuman (2017), and Timothy J. Welsh (2016).

With regard to Kocurek, Avant-Pop can be associated with *Coin-Operated Americans* because of the success with which the author aligns her subject with postmodernism and capitalism, the fertile intellectual soils against which the Avant-Pop emerged. For example, and drawing primarily from David Harvey and Fredric Jameson, Kocurek considers the emergence of the video arcade as being symptomatic of "two major changes in consumer culture" identified by Harvey in his exploration of postmodernity: that is, "a mobilization of fashion in mass markets … and a shift away from a consumption of goods to a consumption of services."[35] These shifts, Kocurek contends, "shortened the lifetime of expenditures and accelerated spending, and enabled a move from an industrial, production-based economy to a service-based, consumer economy."[36] Further, she observes that video gaming may be an example of the "entertainments, spectacles, happenings, and distractions" that Harvey points to in his estimations. To this observation, she brings the notion that Jameson, in his own formulation and consideration of postmodernism, "pinpoints 1973, one year after the release of the first successful commercial video game, as the moment in which postmodernity and late capitalism emerged as dominant cultural and economic forms."[37] In this context, she explores—and explicitly imagines—the videogame arcade as "both a memorial to the modern era and a map to the postmodern age we have come to know as the present—a place we have been and still are."[38]

From an Avant-Pop perspective, the notion that we are in a postmodern age is immediately questionable, and the rationale for such questioning rests on the notion that postmodernity and capitalism have created specific cultural conditions for artistic appropriation that might be resisted via emergent technology. However, it is also the case that *Coin-Operated Americans* does not take the special subject of the artist as an object of prime consideration, so the consideration is essentially external to the author's stated scope. Yet, while Kocurek's acceptance of the postmodern does not fall within the essential conceits of Avant-Pop thought, her extended and persuasive evaluation of capitalism in the postmodern age, delivered in the service of a larger argument on the emergence of the "video gamer as a cultural identity during video gaming's first decade," brings significant meaning to a question that Mark Amerika himself could not have thought to ask in 1992: namely, what were the special cultural conditions of the gamers in the 1980s who would go on to take up the concerns, formally or informally, of the Avant-Pop in the 1990s? This represents a much smaller category of gamer, to be sure, but not necessarily a category of lesser significance. For example, William Gibson, author of texts such as *Johnny Mnemonic* (1981) and *Neuromancer* (1984) which have left a profound and indelible mark on gaming culture, is listed in Amerika's initial list of first-wave Avant-Pop artists.

Such questions have value to game studies beyond the immediate postmodern framework employed in Kocurek's argument. This can be demonstrated with a consideration of Michael Z. Neuman (2017). Instead of the intersection of postmodernism and capitalism, Neuman's title finds its origins in a project for "tracing the history of interactive moving-image technologies, of entwining video game and television history,"[39] and proceeds under the notion that "during their initial period of emergence videogames were objects without fixed meanings, without a clear identity, without a commonly shared understanding of their cultural status."[40] While Neuman makes no reference to the postmodern in his argument, it is generally clear throughout that the notion that videogames emerge as objects "without fixed meanings" is generally referencing the perspective of industrial, capitalist forces, which used the arcade and the home console to profit from the shifting social dynamics of youth culture in the late 1970s and early 1980s. This is underscored by the notion, repeated throughout the text, that the bourgeois markets within which such titles emerged were themselves quite eager to ascribe very particular meaning to these industrial products: for example, they are received as dangerous, disruptive, and debilitating for youth in general and boys in particular, even though—or perhaps indeed because—they were so lucrative.

The tension between these evident forces is a prime feature in Neuman's text, and the author's attention to how these cultural concerns shaped the emergence of new media objects like videogames is admirable. As is the case with Kocurek, the focus throughout is generally on games and gaming culture as experienced by consumers, and the document does not set out or otherwise claim to take up the question of how such concerns and markets might bear on artists. However, it is possible to infer resonances between Neuman's history and the Avant-Pop perspective in Amerika's "Manifesto." For example, and with regard to the values of new media, Amerika sees the emergent Data Superhighway as a means to the end of the same industry pipeline that is so significant to Newman's argument: for example, the chain from author, agent, publisher, printer, distributor, retailer, and consumer. Amerika foresees a direct link between the artist and interactive participants. Importantly, this possibility to "do away with the high-priced middlemen" stands on the notion of artists eager to sample "popular forms of representation" in the service of "dark, sexy, surreal, and subtly ironic gesturing" that resists the "bed of commercial standardization." Such possibility raises questions for Neuman's excellent history, such as whether or not and how the emergence of videogames in America has facilitated new media experiences between artists, receivers, and industry that facilitate Avant-Pop concerns. Moreover, and particularly in light of Kocurek's argument, the question of how games and gaming culture in the 1980s might be regarded as stoking, confronting, or simply eliding industry expectations—for example, "Once Upon a time-ing"—is raised though it remains unaddressed from an Avant-Pop perspective. However, a foundation for such considerations is already present in Neuman's text, as he provides an excellent and detailed consideration of *Pac-Man's* breakthrough popularity with American audiences and explores with some specificity how the seemingly novel features of the title were almost instantaneously (and literally) put into a Nike ad.

The significance of such questions to game studies is underlined by Timothy J. Welsh's (2016) book and is of special relevance to the conclusion of that work. Welsh's argument extends from the author's efforts to fashion a player-centered "critical approach"[41] to videogames, one which attends with some skepticism to immersion metaphors used "to describe the role of media-generated virtualities in everyday life."[42] Beginning with the notion that certain literary theorists and works of literary fiction have grappled with the "immersiveness of fiction" throughout the same decades that witnessed the rise of the videogame industry, Welsh fashions a compelling concept for addressing a specific phenomenon, "mixed realism," which he presents and develops to describe "the ways media-generated virtualities recontextualize the real-world activity of interacting with them."[43] For Welsh, such mixing can occur at multiple levels: for example, the manipulation of a controller to interact with the videogame, as well as (and certainly in a related way) at the level of the plot itself, as in a title like *.hack//infection*, in which the player character must literally play videogames in order to play the videogame *.hack//infection*.

In its totality, Welsh's argument pays significant attention to what he describes as the "postmodern aesthetic" which, Welsh claims, "tracks with the expansion of televisual and digital communication technologies [that] pose questions about the relationship between fiction and reality."[44] This focus, supported by key arguments on self-reflection and metafictional practices in literary fiction and the relevance of these matters to titles as diverse as *Super Columbine Massacre RPG!*, *Prince of Persia: The Sands of Time*, *Eternal Darkness: Sanity's Requiem*, and *Call of Duty: Modern Warfare 2*, establishes an interesting beachhead for future analysis. A specific direction for that analysis is offered in Welsh's concluding chapter, which has a special focus on *Red Dead Redemption*, a title that is of interest to the author because its mixed realism recontextualizes the real-world activity of interacting with it by removing any sort of evident moral compass for valuing the player's act of play, rendering the very concept of preference itself "whimsical," or at the very least promising such an experience while allowing for potential "unguessed kinships" between the player and the objects within the title's amoral landscape.

From an Avant-Pop perspective, these kinships are not "unguessed"—they are the desirable outcomes of efforts to marshal "popularized forms of representation" germane to video gaming in ways that exceed—at a minimum—the "once upon a time-ing" narrative conventions that affirm value-laden social reality. As Kocurek and Neuman make essentially clear, the emergence of videogames in America occurred in the context of contested market values: values for play, values for players, and the construction of industry norms. A game like *Red Dead Redemption* is notable precisely because it rallies select, popularized conventions for play into a sandbox environment that—while not devoid of evident cultural concerns—makes it possible for the player to slip the bonds of "Once upon a time-ing" and wander directly into "exquisite realms of spacy sex and timeless narrative disaster," to an end of confronting consumers with a conundrum: namely, where are the signifiers in the game from which the player can derive meaning? Such vertigo might be regarded as evidence of an a-moral ponderosa and perhaps the fulfillment of the very cultural concerns that early opponents of gaming were panicking over in the press. However, such vertigo might also be evidence of an Avant-Pop sensibility surfacing within plain view of the gaming community, within our common toilet, so to speak. This possibility, which suggests gameplay possibilities that emerge in response to select narrative expectations, can return us to Galloway, for a more extensive consideration of his argument on "congruence."

Game Studies' Postmodern Economics: From Avant-Pop to Social Realism

In November 2004, *Game Studies* published Alexander Galloway's article "Social Realism in Gaming." In that article, Galloway associates broad commentaries on neorealism in cinema and literature with what is supposedly "conventional wisdom"[45] in the popular press on the general benefits and potential dangers of videogames to players.[46] On its own merits, the argument constitutes a herculean task, the nature of which is exposed in the author's rhetorical strategies for establishing a theoretical framework for analysis. An example of such rhetoric and its implications for the author's argument can be identified in Galloway's use of the term "social realism."[47] The path to that term in the essay can be charted through the author's exploration of select claims from Andre Bazin, Fredric Jameson, and Bruno Reichlin. A review of Galloway's approach reveals that, while there is much to celebrate in the essay, the work presents historical fallacies when the author attempts to link these and related claims to videogames. Such moments are productive for the project at hand, as they establish a foundation—and arguably convey a pressing need—for critical attention to poverty thematics in videogames.

For example, on his path to the concept of "social realism," Galloway first attends to Bazin's identification of "realist" in Bazin's broader argument on neorealism in Italian cinema, where Bazin links the term "realist" with "all narrative means tending to bring an added measure of reality to the screen."[48] The identification is sound with respect to Bazin. With that concept for context, Galloway references Fredric Jameson's argument that neorealist cinema tends to convey an essentially socialist perspective in its depictions of life in mid-century Italy, and then Galloway asserts that Bazin and Jameson essentially share the view that the realist aesthetic in neorealism conveys a socialist agenda. While the association of Bazin and Jameson is interesting, it does not lead Galloway to a very robust definition for the functions of such "narrative means" in neorealist subjects. To arrive at that point, he chooses to abandon the cinema altogether and reaches out for Reichlin's description of neorealism in Italian literature: which Reichlin defines as "a surgical examination of matters of society, an almost documentary attention to the everyday, an adherence in thought and language to the social origins and personalities of the characters, a more-or-less direct criticism of current society and morals."

While Galloway's association of Bazin, Jameson, and Reichlin with the concept of neorealism is itself reasoned, even if it does turn a blind eye to the distinctions that might be made between neorealist cinema and literature—and also avoids a deeper reflection on the traceable relevance of socialist thought to and through these arguments. However, these are not necessarily the greatest concerns for scholars following in Galloway's footsteps, as it is also the case that Galloway is less attentive than he might have been to the historical contexts for these arguments. The significance of such contexts is evident in the very next line following Reichlin's definition, which Galloway does not reference. In it, Reichlin identifies an essential cultural context for neorealism in literature, which is to "put the sycophants of the fascist regime on their guard."[49] Mid-century fascism in Italy is also explicitly relevant to Bazin's and Jameson's reflections on Italian cinema, and to their cited comments, but Galloway does not address it as such, and this becomes a significant problem when he simply asserts that "game studies should follow these same arguments and … define realist games as those games that reflect critically on the minutiae of everyday life, replete as it is with struggle, personal drama and injustice."[50] What's missing, of course, is a rationale for why the decidedly twentieth-century neorealist aesthetic, which arises in a specific time and place, should be brought to bear on twenty-first-century subjects.

It is perhaps all too easy to forgive the apparent historical fallacy or to simply overlook it given the state of the field at the time of Galloway's writing. However, it is also the case that the same fallacy returns again in the argument at a crucial moment, at the very point where the author is making his major claims in his discussion of "social realism." For example, his consideration of so-called realist games leads him to assert that such work, to the extent that it offers social critique, is new to gaming in the "twenty-first century." He writes, "Forty years of electronic games have come and gone and only now does one see the emergence of social realism" in games.[51] Crucially, that claim does not stand on the notion that the market is witnessing full-blown titles defined by the described realist aesthetic in 2003 or 2004, but, much more controversially, on the notion that games are simply only then presenting or hinting at such an aesthetic. Consequently, the claim presents a not-to-be-believed historical scope with regard to both the past and the present. Are we simply to assume a broad sensitivity to all games on the part of Galloway? In each of the recent publications I mentioned at the start of this chapter, the notion that the player's act of play is and has been for nearly a half-century a social act, carried out with gaming experiences that very frequently convey complex commentaries on society is plain, as is the notion that the work of identifying and analyzing such commentaries constitutes a rich field for future scholarship.

Yet, the point of re-considering "Social Realism in Gaming" isn't to undermine Galloway's work, but to recognize by comparison the academic environment within which the author chose to reason, as well as the struggle that was undertaken to express a rational observation with limited (and limiting) resources on hand. Precisely because our shared period is one of rich expansion for the field, the question of intellectual contexts is only growing in importance, and not only because it establishes roads for transporting field-specific scholarship to other disciplines, but because it promises paths for receiving insights from other disciplines to game studies. The point takes on special relevance with the publication of two major works, Robert J. Gordon's *The Rise and Fall of American Growth* (2017) and Thomas Piketty's *Capital in the Twenty-First Century* (2014). These works contain novel economic insights with implications for early twenty-first-century scholarship on the rise, spread, and potential growth of gaming cultures in the United States. I will consider the relevant portions of Gordon's and Piketty's interrelated arguments and then will explore some of their exciting implications for Carly A. Kocurek's *Coin-Operated Americans: Rebooting Boyhood at the Video Game Arcade* (2015).

To begin with Gordon, the author labels the period from 1870 to 1970 "the special century" and argues that it was "unique in human history" and "unrepeatable" because "so many of its achievements could happen only once."[52] These achievements include, but are not limited to, improvements to lower- and middle-class dwellings with modifications to sewage systems, the expansion of the electrical grid, and novel devices for refrigeration, as well as general improvements to transportation through the rise of the rail system and advent of the automobile and airplane. Gordon explores in impressive detail the implications of these advancements on "food, clothing, shelter … health, and working conditions both inside and outside of the home" and then comes to the claim that, since the 1970s, "advances have tended to be channeled into a narrow sphere of human activity having to do with entertainment, communications, and the collection and processing of information."[53] While Gordon's definition of "advancement" is somewhat murky, the concept is generally associated with notions of rising quality of life for middle- and low-income individuals, who "advance" to the extent that technological trends remove or lessen the experience of drudgery or unnecessary suffering from their lives.

The document's central premise stands as enticing, potential context for a central claim in another, recent and generally well-received commentary on the modern economy, Piketty's *Capital in the Twenty-First Century* (2014). In that text, Piketty shows with persuasive statistical analysis that the 1970s mark the beginning stages of what has in recent decades transformed into essentially unprecedented levels of wealth inequality in the United States. A central concern in Piketty's analysis is that our current, extended, and remarkable period of economic divergence has so-removed access to wealth and the wealthy from everyday life that these subjects are increasingly understood only as abstractions for the nation's middle-class and impoverished communities. However, when it comes to an actual practical description of how these cultural changes are manifested in everyday life, Piketty is generally silent on the subject. Gordon's argument can bring context to Piketty's major findings, to the extent that it frames the wide and widening gulf between the classes as representing a divergence of access to the fruits of the "special century" that is occurring simultaneously with society-straddling revolutions to entertainment, communications, and information processing.

As *The Rise of Fall of American Growth* and *Capital in the Twenty-First Century* both settle on the Global Great Recession as the essential validation of their analyses of contemporary economics, the promise of these works as context for scholarship within game studies might be illustrated with considerations of economically minded works from the field produced during the post-Recession period. One such work is Kocurek's *Coin-Operated Americans.* The author's compelling "excavation" of the "video gamer as cultural identity during gaming's first decade" attends to, among other things, economic transformations in the 1970s that are particularly relevant to Gordon's comments on advances in entertainment at the end of "the special century."[54] Drawing from David Harvey's *Conditions of Postmodernity*, Kocurek considers two major changes to consumer culture that preceded the widespread rise of the coin-operated videogame industry. She notes Harvey's comments on the "mobilization of fashion in mass (as opposed to elite) markets [which] provided a means to accelerate the pace of consumption not only in clothing, ornament, and decoration but also across a wide swath of life-styles and recreational activities (leisure and sporting habits, pop music styles, video and children's games, and the like)."[55] While Kocurek explores the ramification of this change to daily life in some detail, the relevant point here is that such acceleration contributes to increased economic instability for the involved consumers, with the broader cultural effect of "economic stagnation" in the 1970s. This trend was further compounded by the other major change noted by Harvey and considered by Kocurek, "a shift away from the consumption of goods and into the consumption of services—not only personal, business, educational, and health services, but also into entertainments, spectacles, happenings, and distractions." In the context of Gordon's and Piketty's arguments, these shifts and their impacts on daily life speak to the practical decline of an industrial economy literally unable to keep pace with its own historical trends, while, at the same time, novel opportunities for entertainment become increasingly more enticing possibilities for personal expenditures.

Elsewhere in her argument, Kocurek attends to contextualizing historical forces that can be associated with the beginning of Gordon's "special century" and another significant period in Piketty's modeling of notable periods of rising wealth inequality. She notes the rise of the coin-operated and midway amusements at the end of the nineteenth century and the objections that the period's so-called moral reformers made to lower- and middle-class populations spending their capital on such entertainments. Kocurek writes, "Cheap entertainments were seen as frivolous and wasteful and could be framed as evidence of the working class's poor management of financial resources or of the corrupting influence of such entertainments."[56] Moral arguments aside, in light of Gordon's and Piketty's arguments, such expenditures can now at least partly be understood as the economic activity of people who were, at the moment, locked out of major markets that were starting to advance in historically unprecedented ways even as capital itself was becoming increasingly concentrated in the hands of fewer and fewer people. Thus, at the beginning and end of Gordon's "special century" one encounters people of limited means and limited access to novel technologies for alleviating suffering prioritizing transitory entertainments with their economic activity. As is clear in Kocurek's argument, and other arguments taken on the subject of gaming culture in the 1970s and 1980s, such as Neuman's (2017), the story of gaming in America has not been defined by these populations. However—and as is essentially implied by Galloway—game studies and poverty studies have much to share and learn from each other, and their contextual intersections hold a great deal of promise for future scholarship within and between these fields.

Notes

1. Lesage, 82.
2. Ibid., 93.
3. Ibid., 92.
4. Ibid., 93.
5. Smith 58.
6. Ibid., 73.
7. Ibid., 73.
8. Punday, 94.
9. Pope, "Essay on Man."
10. The Norton Anthology, English Literature, 2226.
11. Orme, "Review."
12. Bak, "Review."
13. Deshane, "Review."
14. MacCallum-Stewart, "Review."
15. Milliam, "Review."
16. Kirkus, "Review."
17. Madden, "Review."
18. Carducci, "Review."
19. McDaniel "Review."
20. https://www.poetryfoundation.org/articles/69379/an-essay-on-criticism
21. Murray, 252.
22. Castronova, *Synthetic* 4097.
23. Wark, 146.
24. Kocurek, 120.
25. Newman, 216.
26. https://www.theguardian.com/books/2014/jul/17/capital-twenty-first-century-thomas-piketty-review
27. https://www.economist.com/the-economist-explains/2014/05/04/thomas-pikettys-capital-summarised-in-four-paragraphs
28. Piketty, 77.
29. Piketty, Chapter II.
30. Kocurek, 737.
31. McCaffery, *Interview.*
32. Ibid.
33. Amerika, *Literary.*
34. Ibid.
35. Kocurek, 700.
36. Ibid., 704.
37. Ibid., 729.

38. Ibid., 381.
39. Newman, 151.
40. Ibid., 220.
41. Welsh, 51.
42. Ibid., 47.
43. Ibid., 360.
44. Ibid., 1583.
45. Galloway, "Social Realism."
46. Ibid.
47. Ibid.
48. Bazin, *What Is....*
49. Reichlin, Figures of Neorealism in Italian Architecture.
50. Galloway, Alexander. "Social Realism in Gaming." *Game Studies: The International Journal of Computer Games Research*. vol 4, issue 1, Nov 2004.
51. Galloway, Social Realism.
52. Gordon, 176.
53. Ibid., 185.
54. Gordon, *Rise and Fall*, Introduction, 1.
55. Kocurek, 701.
56. Kocurek, 1867.

Bibliography

Bogost, Ian. *Persuasive Games: The Expressive Power of Videogames*. Cambridge, Mass: The MIT Press, 2010. Kindle edition.

Castronova, Edward. *Synthetic Worlds: The Business and Culture of Online Games*. Chicago: University of Chicago Press, 2005. Kindle edition.

Chess, Shira. *Ready Player Two: Women Gamers and Designed Identity*. Minneapolis: University of Minnesota Press, 2017. Kindle edition.

Dyer-Witheford, Nick and de Peuter, Greig. *Games of Empire: Global Capitalism and Video Games*. Minneapolis: University of Minnesota Press, 2009. Kindle edition.

Gordon, Robert J. *The Rise and Fall of American Growth*. Princeton: Princeton University Press, 2017. Kindle edition.

Green, Amy M. *Posttraumatic Stress Disorder, Trauma, and History in Metal Gear Solid Five*. Palgrave, 2017. Kindle edition.

"*Hamlet on the Holodeck: The Future of Narrative in Cyberspace*." Kirkus, 1997. https://www.kirkusreviews.com/book-reviews/janet-h-murray/hamlet-on-the-holodeck/.

Harvey, David. *The Conditions of Postmodernity: An Enquiry into the Origins of Cultural Change*. Wiley-Blackwell, 1991.

Kocurek, Carly A. *Coin-Operated Americans: Rebooting Boyhood at the Video Game Arcade* Minneapolis: University of Minnesota Press, 2015. Kindle edition.
Leyner, Mark. *Gone with the Mind.* Little, Brown, 2016. Kindle edition.
McCaffery, Larry. *Avant-Pop: Fiction for a Daydream Nation.* Black Ice Books, 1992
McCaffery, Larry. Avant-Pop: Fiction for a Daydream Nation. Black Ice Books, eds. *After Yesterday's Crash: The Avant-Pop Anthology.* Penguin, 1995.
Neuman, Michael Z. *Atari Age: The Emergence of Video Games in America.* Cambridge, Mass: MIT Press, 2017. Kindle edition.
Nichols, Randy. *The Video Game Business.* British Film Institute, 2014.
Ouellette, Marc A. and Thomson, Jason C. *The Post 9/11 Video Game: A Critical Examination.* McFarland, 2017. Kindle edition.
Piketty, Thomas. *Capital in the Twenty-First Century.* Boston: Harvard University Press, 2014. Kindle edition.
Welsh, Timothy J. *Mixed Realism: Videogames and the Violence of Fiction.* Minneapolis: University of Minnesota Press, 2016. Kindle edition.

CHAPTER 6

Conclusion

Literary Contexts for Digital Slumming

In the previous chapters, we have considered select rhetorical and conceptual practices in key academic works associated with game studies. While this consideration has been far from exhaustive of the field's many and varied contributions, it has hopefully provided some sense of the field-in-development during the early twenty-first century. It would be an overstatement to argue that the concept of poverty has been central to such works. However, as we have touched on the various discursive practices that scholars have deployed to address the subject or related subjects, we have hopefully gained a broader appreciation for the kinds of thinking that have been central to the field's development to date. More broadly, we have gained an understanding of what is at stake in scholarship on games, gamers, and gaming communities—that is, the human subject and its interrelations with digital entertainments.

With respect to the concept of poverty, this review has repeatedly stressed the notion that discourse on the subject stands in want of a contextualizing frame that exceeds the digital experience. It has been argued that the need for such a frame (or frames) is warranted by the player's act of play—a subject at the heart of common enterprise, which itself stands on the notion that the act of play is activity and aggressively shaped by the fluxing contexts of the player and the played. The transmedia subject of slumming has been used at many turns as just such a frame, in order to add

A. Crowley, *Representations of Poverty in Videogames*,
https://doi.org/10.1007/978-3-031-00144-4_6

new definition to well-established concepts like congruence and virtual poverty. Slumming, of course, is not necessarily the only frame for such analysis—but it is a frame for such analysis. While slumming is a useful concept for describing the enacting of play—that is, the movement of the player into and then out of an impoverished or impoverishing experience—it is also true that this movement comes with what might be generally called narrative expectations. That is, the movement into, though, and out of the slum occurs for the purpose of providing the slumming individual a view of a promised experience with some manifestation of destitution. With respect to game studies' general body of scholarship, this is perhaps the aspect of slumming that is at once most difficult to reconcile with the field and also the most necessary aspect to be reconciled. This is because slumming assumes narrative expectations that inform the experience but are not wholly descriptive of any given instance of slumming.

The concept of poverty thematics, which has been addressed at multiple points in the preceding chapters, essentially stands on the assumption that the features of slumming undergird various facets of play that organize players' in-game socioeconomic experiences. While it may not be the case that slumming needs to play this role in any given gaming experience, the notion throughout this book has been that it certainly can be and is with respect to the relevant titles considered so far. However, what has not yet been attended to is an argument that calls out by name the analytical concepts that describe the union of a slumming conceit with a poverty thematic. This is no accident, and the silence so far has a field-specific justification, which I will address in the following pages. Fortunately, and as we will see, this issue also has a field-specific solution.

Literary Studies: Game Studies' Coalmine Canary

The decade following the Global Great Recession witnessed a meaningful shift within game studies. This shift involved a movement away from grand efforts to define the videogame form—as evident in early work from Janet Murray, McKenzie Wark, and Edward Castronova—and toward considerations of the player's act of play, as evident in recent work from, among others, Mary Flanagan and Helen Nissenbaum, Katherine Isbister, Mark A. Ouellette, and Jason C. Thompson. A rationale for this shift can be located in two recession-era texts: Castronova's *Exodus to the Virtual World* (2007) and Nick Dyer-Witheford and Greig de Peuter's *Games of*

Empire (2009), both of which offer salient and persuasive points on the videogame form while oftentimes laboring to explain the relevance of the form to the world's markets and governments. Regarding Castronova, such language can be associated with his earnest assertion that "fun will become a core objective of our society"[1]—an assertion that stands on the author's own, lightly detailed conception of "fun" paired with an essentially superficial conception of society—one that lacks, for example, any significant awareness of class stratification, inherited wealth, or the intergenerational transmission of poverty. Regarding Dyer-Witheford and de Peuter, such language can be associated with statements that, unlike those found in Castronova, wholeheartedly embrace the dismal language of economic reality. Readers are told, for example, that "the inhabitants of *Second Life* are…class-divided, property-owning, commodity-exchanging, currency-trading, networking, energy-consuming subjects of a comprehensively capitalist order."[2] While that claim and similar claims are certainly reasonable, what's missing in *Games of Empire* is a data-driven explanation of and for that capitalist order, especially as it bears on the context of *Second Life* and similar titles—beyond data that is gleaned from shareholder reports for major gaming corporations, and earnest, twentieth-century theories on the concept of empire itself.

To be sure, in their respective rhetorical contexts, *Exodus to the Virtual World* and *Games of Empire* offer revelatory and field-expanding commentaries on games and gamers, but their engagement with the broader world, usually communicated through economic prognostications directed at our shared moment and beyond, is tenuous if not simply exhausting. An explanation for such exhaustion is expressed in at least two major works that have emerged in response to the Global Great Recession: Thomas Piketty's *Capital in the Twenty-First Century* (2014) and Robert J. Gordon's *The Rise and Fall of American Growth* (2017). One relevant conclusion that can be drawn from the sobering statistical data in these titles is that, in the foreseeable future, the notion that our remarkable period of extraordinary wealth inequality will be either corrected or exacerbated by the videogame form is simply irrational. In short, the challenge that form-focused titles like *Exodus to the Virtual World* and *Games of Empire* face is a problem of scope, if not humility.

Should scope and humility be reasonable concerns in notable contributions to game studies in the pre- and intra-Great Recession periods, then it is reasonable to ask if there are any discernible rhetorical trends in earlier, significant scholarship that may have set the stage for such discourse.

Without pointing too many fingers, it should be noted that literary studies has played and continue to play a meaningful role in the development of game studies as an academic discipline. While the point is surely arguable, the uses and abuses of the field in pre-Global Great Recession scholarship might now, in retrospect, be regarded as something of a canary in the coalmine, in terms of the complications some theorists encountered when attempting to carry their formal arguments into the wider world and especially into corners of the world traditionally concerned with academic discourse on literary subjects. Take for example Janet Murray's expansive catalogue of literary examples in *Hamlet on the Holodeck*, marshaled to support her central thesis "that computation offers a powerful new set of expressive affordances for the ancient human activity of storytelling." Authors as diverse as William Shakespeare, Italo Calvino, and Charlotte Bronte find themselves shoulder-to-shoulder not only with one another but also with *Zork*, *Tetris*, and *King's Quest*, and all are united under patchwork references to broad theoretical concerns derived from Jean Baudrillard, Walter Benjamin, and Marshall McLuhan. Without objecting to Murray's thesis or even to her essential approach, one of the most telling features of *Hamlet on the Holodeck* is its significant investment in critical approaches to narrativity and narrative theory over scholarship on the specific literary works and authors the author mentions along the way. One effect of this in writing is that the author simply moves on from her references to specific authors and titles without resolving their essential significance to the assumptions from narrative theory that constitute the backbone of the project. For example, early in the document Murray makes use of Aldous Huxley's *Brave New World* and Ray Bradbury's *Fahrenheit 451* as solid evidence of "a widely read dystopian tradition [that] depicts futuristic entertainment forms as intrinsically degrading."[3] While the claim is not false, none of the nuance or intellectual specificity of that tradition is included in Murray's argument, as the author does not offer any appeals to scholarship concerned with such matters. While there is no reason not to take her word for it, we should notice that we are being *asked* to take her word for it.

One of the interesting consistencies in post-Recession titles taken with the player's act of play, including those mentioned at the beginning of this chapter, is that they are noticeably less invested in literary studies, either as context for or as essential substance within their arguments. Carly A. Kocurek's *Coin-Operated Americans* and Michael Z. Neuman's *Atari Age: The Rise of Video Games in America* showcase how the field can flourish without direct investment in literary studies. With distinct insights, the authors present compelling histories of the development of gaming culture and identity in the United States, with a scholarly focus that extends from the late nineteenth century to the present. With only minor exceptions, these authors essentially do not attend to the topic of literary context when exploring the rise of gaming as a form of entertainment within the United States. This is particularly noteworthy when the authors return at several points to broad cultural conversations on the objectionable nature of gaming and how its rise came at the apparent expense of more traditional forms of entertainment, such as novel reading. To be sure, their silence on such matters is not a shortcoming in either argument, as these texts have clear and persuasive theoretical boundaries for commentary. In the broader context of game studies, with its troubled history of half-measures with regard to literary subjects, these arguments compel an unsettling question: what actual use is literary studies to game studies, and—as a related question—what use is game studies to literary studies?

Fortunately, productive answers to both these questions can be found in Timothy J. Welsh's *Mixed Realism: Videogames and the Violence of Fiction* (2016), which identifies a modest, promising, and much-needed trajectory for scholarship concerned with the intersection of game studies and literary studies. The author establishes a clear and bounded theoretical framework for analysis, centered on a postmodern aesthetic associated in all or part with a short list of during-their-time avant-garde authors—such as Truman Capote, Thomas Pynchon, Robert Coover, Jon Barth, David Foster Wallace, and Cormac McCarthy—and then explores in detail the significance of the narrative techniques in such works to the player's act of play in titles including but not limited to *Super Columbine Massacre RPG!*, *Call of Duty: Modern Warfare 2*, and *Red Dead Redemption*. Importantly, such detailing succeeds in elevating the identified aesthetic itself over the individual literary and gameplay instances that are explored in the document, to an effect of inviting—if not compelling—future scholarly inquiry into the author's reasoned concerns, rather than into boundless possibilities.

The work and its implications for future scholarship can be contextualized through comparison with Darshana Jayemanne's equally notable and exciting *Performativity in Art, Literature, and Videogames* (2017) which offers a "comparative approach to the analysis of videogame performances"[4] and an internal methodology designed to account for the many ways that performances arise within videogames.[5] The argument's broad theoretical foundation is matched in scope only by its potentially enormous catalogue of professed future applications, which are, according to the author, offered in anticipation of as-of-yet unimagined so-called electric bodies that may be rendered under distant technological advances. Without diminishing or even objecting to Jayemanne's vision of future relevance, it is interesting to note that, by comparison, Welsh is offering something quite distinct: a generally (and chronologically) defined aesthetic movement and its possible associations with a discreet constellation of isolated titles. While his offering contains a number of notable comments on the titles themselves, its larger and perhaps more important implication can be found in its underlying concern with the player's act of play. Over the course of the document, the many and varied levels of narrative complexity associated with the player's act of play imply the act is a site of converging as well as emerging aesthetic concerns that contribute to extremely nuanced cultural developments. In short, Welsh is humanizing, rather than universalizing, the player's act of play. And he is doing it with novels.

In addition to its limited and comparatively humble scope, *Mixed Realism* can also be distinguished from other noteworthy contributions to game studies by its particular approach to postmodernism and postmodern aesthetics. For example, Kocurek's *Coin-Operated Americans* (2015) identifies and advances a particular conception of the postmodern and its relevance to late twentieth-century economics that draws in significant ways from David Harvey's *The Conditions of Postmodernity: An Enquiry into the Origins of Cultural Change*. With excellent analysis, Kocurek extracts key insights from Harvey and associates them with the development of the coin-operated markets in North America, in ways that expand the understanding of her chosen subject matter and its possible implications for Harvey's argument. Welsh's engagement with a postmodern aesthetics pulls the argument toward a less certain set of central suppositions than the set that is evident in *Coin-Operated Americans*. Indeed, a review of the document does not lead to any one particular conception of the postmodern itself, but rather to a set of literary examples that have associations with a diverse set of concerns that are themselves associated with a range of sometimes intersecting and other times less obviously reconcilable reflections on postmodern thought and aesthetics. This is not to say that Welsh's approach is boundless, but rather it proceeds under a general logic of illuminating instances of possible association, in the service of expanding general awareness of postmodern thought itself, and not under the notion that such illuminations must necessarily be brought to order under a determined and particular postmodern agenda.

Limited in its scope and associative in its logic, the argument achieves its stated goal of articulating a critical approach to games and the player's act of play that gives "players a little more credit" with respect to their assumed levels of narrative literacy.[6] The work indicates a meaningful path for future inquiries into the intersection of literary studies and game studies: that is, what are the literary contexts for games, and what are the gaming contexts for literature. This path does not disavow the notion that these contexts may be contexts-in-kind in our common period, though it does underscore the notion that great work remains to be done on the subject of these fields and their possible associations.

Immediate direction for such scholarship can be inferred from Kocurek's and Newman's texts, which present rationales for the rise of gaming in adolescent and teenage populations in the 1970s. What were the literary contexts for *Pong*, *Pac-Man*, *Space Invaders*, and *Centipede*? Excellent work on interactive fiction, such as *Adventure* and *Zork*, already addresses the significance of high and low fantasy to text-based titles, but what might be said about the players who came to gaming through home console experiences? The history of game scholarship suggests that the question can lead to a trap: that is, to begin with too broad assumptions about the players or their gaming experiences. Welsh's argument suggests a different direction: namely, to first identify a mature aesthetic movement with literacy exemplars. With regard to Welsh's own approach, the period of the 1970s offers some practical challenges for analysis, as a number of the major works Welsh uses to defend and clarify his approach come from later decades. This is not to suggest that his argument is necessarily invalidated by works from the 1970s, but the time period raises practical concerns that beg consideration and call out for scholarship that will ascertain if the postmodern aesthetic can be traced through the 1970s across the spines of novels, but also—and perhaps most importantly—if there are other interesting literary traditions that might contribute to this work.

Gentility and the Intersection of Game Studies and Literary Studies

How, then, might scholarly interested in representations of poverty in videogames build on the work and conceptional possibilities offered by authors like Welsh, Jayemanne, and Kocurek? Earlier, I explored the relevance of a transmedia concept, slumming, to the player's act of play. Select literary values associated with transmedia, North American notions of gentility can be used to a similar effect—that is, to frame and describe the collision of particular aesthetic sensibilities with the player's act of play. Values for such work can be inferred from much of what has been best and worst in early twenty-first-century popular press coverage of games, gamers, and gaming—which has lurched from the essentially absurd (e.g., the uninformed and simply confusing "divide" between ludology and narratology) to the absolutely tragic (e.g., patterns of sexual harassment as typified by "gamergate" and related controversies). At the moment, the significance of such commentary to digital storytelling is an open question. For example, it is one thing—and a good thing—to note the lack of scholarly rigor in whole cloth comparisons of "ludology" and "narratology," as such notations affirm the integrity of either field and their potential collaborative values for scholarship on storytelling, digital or otherwise. Moreover, and with an eye to gamergate and all forms of discrimination and marginalization, it is hard to imagine the critical value of any commentary that fails to advance the essential humanist values that have shaped the discourse on society in all its formulations—analog, digital, or otherwise—since the time of the Renaissance.

A rationalization for how academic bodies invested in literary traditions might make such matters useful for analyses can be found in George Santayana's conception of "gentility." As described by Santayana in 1911, the term is generally used to describe transatlantic middle-class efforts to engage and affirm that which is "best" in society, under the auspices of a Victorian social perspective.[7] Traditional scholarship on the subject regards the American experience of the genteel tradition as a late nineteenth-century, early twentieth-century phenomenon, which concludes with the First World War and the emergence of industrial markets and the dissolution of the Victorian ideals that sustained particular conceptions of comportment and discrimination in commerce. However, this notion has been challenged with some success by Joan Shelley Rubin in *The Making of Middlebrow Culture* (1992). Rubin considers how the emergence of mass media in the postwar years enabled the genteel tradition to live on in a "chastened and redirected" form in new characterizations of the ideal consumer.[8] For Rubin, these characterizations contain both the best and worst elements of gentility: they educate people on how to live, but that education is not concerned with a sustainable model for human happiness. Thus, Rubin argues, we are in a "race between [virtual] education and [actual] catastrophe" and are losing sight of the "moral and aesthetic commitments which the makers of the of middlebrow culture at their best tried to diffuse."[9]

In terms of our common moment, one of the chief aesthetic commitments of the middlebrow—as discussed by Rubin—is the commitment to a transmedia perspective, utilized to associate that which is best in a subject—game or otherwise—with a broad catalogue of artistic creations from a range of cultures and historical periods. It demands a broad and ever-broadening cultural perspective, pursued under the assumption that great works can emerge in any medium and that their very greatness stems from their capacity to identify and re-align in imaginative ways the ideas of the day with the ideas that have sustained the world since antiquity. This would be a central assumption that would underlie any answer to the question of what it is, exactly, to be valued in digital storytelling, if the answer to that question is relevant to scholarly conceptions of beauty and truth—that is, aesthetics. Foundational and particular arguments for this perspective can be found in works by John Stuart Mill and Matthew Arnold, and they are worthy of a quick review.

An Aesthetic Tradition for Literary Considerations of the Player's Act of Play

Writing in 1833, Mill famously divorces the term "poetry" from its traditional associations with verse and prose and argues that poetry is a transmedia artistic effect with the capacity to paint "the human soul truly."[10] As such, Mill argues, it may exist "in prose as well as verse" and also in "the audible symbols called musical sounds" and "even through the language of sculpture, painting and architecture."[11] Mill is generally silent on the personal or social conditions that facilitate the production of poetic works, but he does note that poetry is "the natural fruit of solitude and meditation; eloquence, of intercourse with the world."

Writing a little over thirty years later, Matthew Arnold considers the nature of such intercourse as it might be related to what he deems truly masterful productions, which, in his estimation, require the concurrence of "the power of the man" (i.e., the artist) and "the power of the moment."[12] Arnold contends that the artist must grasp and give new expression to the ideas and thoughts that both inform the age and, simultaneously, the ideas and thoughts that connect the age to previous and grand civilizations. According to Arnold, this requires either great reading or great exposure to "fresh thought, intelligent and alive" with broad historical significance.[13] Arnold's notions were generally embraced in the early United States, largely by populations who responded to the assumption that social relevance could be acquired through the consideration of ideas, rather than—as had traditionally been the case for East Coast Gentry prior to and immediately following the Revolution—the acquisition of material goods for display: for example, textiles, china, and other refinements.

Interestingly, Arnold arrives at his position by impugning literary works and social conditions with special relevance to digital storytelling in the contemporary period. First, he argues that many of the progenitors of what would go on to become the gothic tradition—Byron, Shelley, and, to a lesser extent, Coleridge—failed to produce great literature because they failed to read enough to understand the great ideas that gave shape to their age—and for Arnold these ideas had an uncomfortably close cataclysmic expression in the French Terror. Thus, such works are "empty of matter," "incoherent," and "so wanting in completeness and variety," because they fail—in his estimation—to address what actually matters in the moment.[14] Roughly two centuries of criticism would suggest that Arnold vastly undervalued these authors and their writing. However, his apparent error does not disprove his essential point: that is, works should be valued for their greater contributions to societies across time, which, for Arnold, would be an illumination of what Mill calls "the human soul," the contours of which may, in Arnold's case at least, exceed the vision of a given critic.[15]

Rubin explains that, on the American front, the Arnoldian call for adequate reading and cultural exposure played into a number of emerging markets that promised those with the luxury of "solitude and meditation" with an "intercourse with the world" through guided reading programs, book clubs, lecture circuits, and the like.[16] While such enterprises were novel to the American scene, it is also the case that, in the context of

Northrop Frye's consideration of popular literature in *The Secular Scripture: The Structure of Sentimental Romance* (1978), there was nothing essentially new about them. Frye addresses conceptions of popular literature that regards such works as "masturbatory" distractions that appeal to those who are least informed or the those who have the worst dispositions. He explores the significance of such hierarchical thinking to the broad history of the Judeo-Christian tradition and works to redeem such "distractions" by associating them with a grand and extended literary genre: the sentimental romance.[17] In recent work, David M. Leeson has made an interesting connection between Frye's conception of sentimental romance and story structure in videogames, under the assumption that many popular titles follow the general contours of the romantic narrative, as defined by Frye. While limited, the argument represents a deliberate effort to regard the potential "poetic" values of digital storytelling in videogames from a critical perspective with transmedia implications.[18] This work is emerging at what just may be the perfect moment in time for considerations of how games can be connected to broader social concerns with decided genteel values—that is, such values as they relate to what is considered to be "the best" in contemporary society.

For example, Thomas Piketty provides novel economic insight on a unifying cultural concern with relevance to the work of Mill and Arnold and also to the later American purveyors of culture and character. Piketty provides some of the most accurate data on wealth inequality in the Western world over the last three centuries. His work concerns notable economic transformations for the United States, the United Kingdom, and France. All three experienced radical transformations in the distribution of wealth in the immediate pre-Victorian and pre-Great War years and also in the contemporary global recession of 2007–2009. With regard to the contemporary period, Piketty posits that for many, the "inescapable reality is this: wealth is so concentrated that a large segment of society is virtually unaware of its existence so that some people imagine that it belongs to surreal or mysterious entities."[19] This notion has strong resonance with the criticism of M0ill and Arnold, to the extent that it suggests people must be educated on the subject if they are to live their best lives. Moreover, and surprisingly, like Mill and Arnold, Piketty contends that the best way to illustrate these realities is with the literature of the day, which should be scoured for its significance to other times.

One of the key tenants in Piketty's argument is that historically literature has functioned as a forum for societies to view their collective understandings of capital, commerce, and the market's finer offerings—but, he argues, that tradition essentially came to an end with the First World War. While he does not address the genteel tradition, one of the great unanswered questions of his argument is whether or not—and how—literature might foreground a culture's conceptions of capital and commerce—even if those conceptions are skewed in peculiar ways by the reality-warping effects of massive income inequality. This question leads to an answer that might be used to bridge the seventy-five-year span that separates the end of Rubin's argument from the conclusion of Piketty's: the emergence of digital entertainment, generally—and digital storytelling in games, specifically.

Construed broadly—from their earliest location-locked manifestations as business simulators in Albuquerque, New Mexico, in the 1950s to the catalogue of globally distributed, persistent titles of the present—such games have a significant relationship with wealth—and in particular conspicuous wealth. While certain examples from the post-gaming industry bust of the early 1980s may leap to mind—for example, coins with value toward an extra life in *Super Mario Brothers*, or rupees exchanged for items in *The Legend of Zelda*—it is the case that a number of earlier works also unfold with one eye on adventure and one on wealth: items gathered for use in *Zork* and multiple forms of capital in the earliest text-based iterations of *The Oregon Trail*. Moreover, and moving even further into the past, one cannot but help be struck by the significance of numerical "points" to *Pong*, or *Computer Space*, which speak to—and essentially come to represent through indicating—the player's history of play. Moreover, conceptions of wealth and extraordinary wealth would also seem to be relevant to the earliest tiles, such as *Spacewar!*, which—while lacking points in its earliest manifestations—illustrated the combat of fantastical space vehicles at a time with the formation and, importantly, cost of far more humble machines that were central to the American experience.

Certainly, these conceptions of wealth in games are not offered to indicate that wealth has one function or a limited set of functions in these titles. However, a broader consideration of games that moves into the current period can notice what appears to be the ever-broadening and ever-more granular representation of not only capital in videogames but capital with ready and easy associations with what it is that is supposedly "the best" in the game or games under consideration. For example, in the games explored so far in this book, capital is literally the road to story, and a relative absence of capital is literally the context for future play. What we know from Piketty's economic charts and from industry data, like the kind provided by the Entertainment Software Rating Board (ESRB), is that the very players who are most invested in such circumstances are statistically the same group of players who are becoming ever more removed from the experience of wealth and more associated with poverty in contemporary life. That is, they are, according to Piketty, very likely to associate wealth and the wealthy with "surreal and mysterious entities." Considerations of poverty and its possible association with representations of romance and excellence in digital storytelling have the capacity to uncover a link between the player, the played, and criticism and commentary relevant to the ages.

A Point of Departure for Literary Considerations of the Player's Act of Play: "Lore"

Such work might begin with a consideration of "lore." While earlier instances may exist, the special use of "lore" to denote culturally specific knowledge and traditions within digital communities—artificial or otherwise—appears to have first emerged at the turn of the century, where it can be found in commentary on Blizzard Entertainment's *Diablo*. In its early instances, the term appears with some regularity on the fan-based website *Blizzplanet*, in posts that detail the historical contexts or further adventures of key characters in the then-developing *Diablo* franchise. *Blizzplanet* was and remains a site maintained by franchise fans, and many of the early "lore" postings read as straight fan-fiction: authors with fantastical pen names such as Medeivaldragon post on topics as diverse as "the nature of soulstones," the history of the fantasy city of Stormwind, and the player classes that populate Blizzard's various worlds.

This use of "lore" to describe both the fantasy elements of the game and the practical strategies that players might employ to improve a gameplay experience have a corresponding use in simultaneous discussions of pen and paper role-playing games. Again, while earlier instances may exist, it is in this exact same period that initial references to "lore" in *Dungeons and Dragons* begin to emerge with some frequency online. Here, too, the point of origin appears to be fan-sites, such as *enworld*, with the earliest instances emerging in commentary on the *Ravenloft Forbidden Lore* boxed set. There, as is the case with the early *Blizzplanet* instances, "lore" is used to convey something that might be termed a "selective but practical history" of the game in question: it holds the promise of more than a broadened cultural appreciation for the imagined community under investigation. It also conveys a set of practices and expectations that arrive with the promise of facilitating gameplay to the end of player achievement both in the instance of play and in the player's capacity to imagine him or herself as an actor in a grand—and detailed—narrative that exceeds his or her act of play.

Lore as such typically marshals a cultural history to the service and aid of gameplay, and this effect has its own history of development in the final decades of the twentieth century in transmedia subjects. For example, this relationship finds a rather well-developed expression in a series of novels that actually preceded the widespread use of "lore" as such. In the late 1970s, 1980s, and 1990s, publishing house TRS released some 242 *Dungeons and Dragons* novels, which tended to be released in anticipation of—or in support of—a gaming product concerned with the same essential elements of these narratives. Interestingly, this relationship between a determined "stage setting" for future narrative endeavors also has a rather significant cultural realization in other media at the turn of the century, within continuing significance into the present period, and is evidenced by the emergence of the "prequel" and its distant cousin the "reboot" or "refresh" in cinema at the same time. The "prequel," of course, has special—if arguably tragic—significance to the *Star War* franchise at the turn of the millennium, both in terms of the critical failures like *The Phantom Menace*, but also in the exceedingly "TRS-esque" series of novels that preceded the film to provide "added context" to the viewer's experience.

In the context of game studies and critical commentary on digital literature, one cannot help but notice the term's significance to (and perhaps very early solution to) the decade-long scholarly hiccup that was the so-called debate between "ludology" and "narratology," insofar as "lore" establishes a certain expectation: namely, that story elements have significance to play in ways that exceed their realization in the player's gaming and that this significance extends into the historical conditions that undergird play itself. In this context, the player's gaming—his or her interaction with contextually significant people, places, and things—literally carries with it the weight of the world and can be conceptualized with various levels of specificity with respect to that world. With regard to first-wave ludology, a pressing question can be derived from this relationship: namely, whether or not and how any game-based action with significance to the world at hand can be divorced from not just game history but also the narrative of that history as it bears on the moment of action, regardless of whether it is significant at the moment of the action's execution. It is not until rather recently that such critics have come around to the perhaps all-too-obvious conclusion: it cannot be divorced.

Assessing Lore's Significance to Relative Poverty

In his *Narrative Discourse: An Essay in Method*, Gérard Genette provides some useful terms for exploring such contextualization. Speaking in terms of the role of flashback (or analepsis) in fiction, Genette considers a range of artistic possibilities for expanding diegetic content with homodiegetic (i.e., similar to established) or heterodiegetic (i.e., distinctive from established) content. While the chief effect of such context is to expand upon the established world that is represented in a given narrative, it also—for Genette—has significant implications for the concept of voice, which he defines as the distinction between the enunciator and the enunciated: that is to say, between the speaker and what it is that the speaker actually says. Considered in this way, one of the interpretive and artistic effects of "lore" is to highlight—or otherwise raise questions about—the method and manner in which new diegetic content is introduced as lore, and its bearing on established content.

Genette's chief concern in the consideration of these subjects is the representation of time: the time of the established content and the time of the added content, and how they are joined through artistic or merely practical methods to facilitate the reader's temporal perspective. It is interesting to note that "lore" in the context of the titles considered so far demands a homodiegetic perspective: that is to say, it stands as an elaboration upon a place, person, or event that the player has or will encounter—in person or through some sort of reference—in the course of normal play. The intertextual references are ready and deliberately spaced. As a design, such narrative would seem to resonate very strongly with Northrop Frye's conception of how a narrative universe can emerge from a simple and perhaps isolated fairy-tale or more developed prose romance. He notes how such works can begin to "stick together" in the course of normal cultural dissemination and how they establish a potentially massive self-referential system, which would—to use Genette's term—turn on its homodiegetic associations and intertextual junctions.

From Genette and Frye, then, one might conclude that there is nothing very surprising about the emergence of online "lore" bearing on videogame titles. Indeed, it is interesting to note how fashionable the term has become in the games industry and at precisely a time when that industry is growing so rapidly. For example, it now is possible to find references to lore as such in titles as diverse as *Mass Effect* and *Animal Crossing*. Podcasts, vlogs, and numerous web-based media dedicated to "lore" have sprung up in the last decade, and the term is only rivaled in its industry saturation by the strange new use of "universe"—to convey the notion of associated franchises emerging under a branded title: for example, the "Marvel" or "DC" universe. Given the prevalence of lore in the contemporary gamespace, it is reasonable to ask whether or not—and to what extent—a poetics of lore might be determined. That is to say, are we starting to see codified practices for the enunciation of lore within specific titles and properties, and are these practices emblematic of a certain kind of voice, or chorus of voices? And, with respect to the subject of this book, might such practices be relatable to conceptions of relative poverty and digital slumming?

For example, let's return for a moment to *The Elder Scrolls V: Skyrim*, as the title is useful for making the point. There are over 800 "books and documents" that can be read on *Skyrim*. However, there are actually many more books scattered across the game space—in the form of originals and duplicates, and many "ruined books," that simply cannot be read. While the game contains libraries and other storage sites for literary documents, one of the most interesting aspects of play with respect to relative poverty is how common books are across Skyrim. In caves, dungeons, keeps, glens, and cemeteries, books are literally laying around and waiting to be read. In Chap. 1, I noted how the market economy of *Skyrim* operated without apparent attention to location-specific economic factors—such as the challenges of selling goods in a slum or, say, on top of a mountain. The abundance of literary documents in *Skyrim* suggests the game unfolds in a region with enormous levels of literacy, untroubled by any location-specific education factors (e.g., a near total lack of schools). Between books and markets, the game expresses the notion that location itself does not necessarily determine the material conditions of play.

With respect to what those documents actually say, they could all reasonably be associated with the notion of lore as it has been addressed so far. However, the context of relative poverty can be used to focus a player's reading of these same documents, to the extent that the reading involves attention to the ways in which *Skyrim*'s literary documents individually and collectively detail standards of living that are specific to particular societies with relevance to the player's acts of play. For the moment, the extent to which such information may or may not be found in the documents is of less relevance than the notion that in-game lore might be approached as a literary subject that can contribute to a developed or developing sense of economic conditions with relevance—atmospheric or otherwise—to the player's acts of play. This valuation of in-game literature might be reasonably extended to written materials that emerge in any number of games considered so far.

However, even as a possible valuation for in-game literature emerges, it is important to consider that most of the books in Skyrim cannot actually be read. These "ruined books" are the most common type of document in the game, and they have special value for the literary concerns considered so far. For example, the ruined books cannot—at least through their evident content—contribute to refined, lore-specific understandings of the game. However, their basic presence in the game is in and of itself significant to the notion of relative poverty. These texts emerge most frequently in spaces that are less than desirable for the storage or upkeep of print literature—in caves, in the forest, left in the open at encampments. As such, they represent notions of lack of care or abandonment—of processes for holding that have resulted in deterioration. On the one hand, such deteriorations add to the mystique of Skyrim, as the player is left to wonder what the books might have said or could have said. However, and perhaps more importantly, the ruined books affirm the general relevance of the written word to Skyrim, across what can generally be described as all kinds of settlements, regardless of the cultural conditions of the settlements themselves. They suggest that books, ruined or not, are central to the game's economic topography: Skyrim has a literary landscape that is interwoven with and indeed is a central feature of its broader environmental concerns. A review of that landscape and its implications for *Skyrim*'s poor and impoverished communities stands as a critical opportunity for the arguments offered in this book.

Notes

1. Castronova, 2941.
2. Dyer-Witheford, 119.
3. Murray, 18.
4. Jayemanne, 2.
5. Ibid., 20.
6. Welsh, 51.

7. Rubin, 172.
8. Ibid., 189.
9. Ibid., 350.
10. Mills, Norton.
11. Ibid.
12. Arnold, Norton.
13. Ibid.
14. Ibid.
15. Ibid.
16. Rubin, *Middlebrow.*
17. Frye, 1007.
18. Leeson.
19. Piketty, 259.

Bibliography

Dyer-Witheford, Nick and de Peuter, Greig. *Games of Empire: Global Capitalism and Video Games.* Minneapolis: University of Minnesota Press, 2009. Kindle edition.

Gordon, Robert J. *The Rise and Fall of American Growth.* Princeton: Princeton University Press, 2017. Kindle edition.

Jayemanne, Darshana. *Performativity in Art, Literature, and Videogames.* Palgrave Macmillan, 2017. Kindle edition.

Kocurek, Carly A. *Coin-Operated Americans: Rebooting Boyhood at the Video Game Arcade* Minneapolis: University of Minnesota Press, 2015. Kindle edition.

Rubin, Joan Shelley. *The Making of Middlebrow Culture.* Chapel Hill: University of North Caroline Press, 1992. Kindle edition.

Bibliography

3rd World Farmer. Common Sense Media, 2005.

Aarseth, Espen. *Cybertext: Perspectives on Ergodic Literature*. Baltimore: John Hopkins University Press, 1997.

Amerika, Mark "Avant-Pop Manifesto: Thread Bearing Itself in Ten Quick Posts." 1992. https://literarymovementsmanifesto.wordpress.com/.

Anderson, Benedict. *Imagined Communities: Reflections on the Origins and Spread of Nationalism*. Verso, 1983.

Anderson-Barkley, Taylor and Kira Foglesong, "Activism in Video Games: A New Voice for Social Change." *Woke Gaming: Digital Challenges to Oppression and Social Injustice*. Eds. Kishonna Gray and David J. Leonard. Seattle: University of Washington Press, 2018. 252–269.

Bak, Meredith A. Review of *Coin-Operated Americans: Rebooting Boyhood at the Video Game Arcade*, by Carly A. Kocurek. *The Journal of the History of Childhood and Youth* 10, no. 1 (2017): 145–147. https://doi.org/10.1353/hcy.2017.0017.

Bazin, André. *What is Cinema? Volume II*. Berkeley, University of California Press, 1971.

Bogost, Ian. *Persuasive Games: The Expressive Power of Videogames*. Cambridge, Mass: The MIT Press, 2010. Kindle edition.

Butler, J. 2009. "Performativity, Precarity and Sexual Politics." *AIBR: Revista de antropologia iberoamericana* 4 (3) 2009: 1–3.

Carducci, Vince. "Gamer Theory – a successor paradigm." *Harvard University Press Blog*, 2007. https://harvardpress.typepad.com/hup_publicity/2007/06/gamer_theorya_s.html.

A. Crowley, *Representations of Poverty in Videogames*,
https://doi.org/10.1007/978-3-031-00144-4

Carr, Diane. "Play Dead: Genre and Affect in *Silent Hill* and *Planescape Torment*" *Game Studies: The International Journal of Computer Game Research* 3, No. 1 (May 2003).

Castronova, Edward. *Synthetic Worlds: The Business and Culture of Online Games*. Chicago: University of Chicago Press, 2005. Kindle edition.

Castronova, Edward. *Exodus to the Virtual World: How Online Fun is Changing Reality*. Palgrave Macmillan, 2007. Kindle edition.

Chang, Alenda. *Playing Nature: Ecology in Video Games*. Minneapolis: University of Minnesota Press, 2019. Kindle edition.

Chess, Shira. *Ready Player Two: Women Gamers and Designed Identity*. Minneapolis: University of Minnesota Press, 2017. Kindle edition.

Chokshi, Niraj. 'Why Gamers Are Protesting BlizzCon for Hong Kong' (New York Times, 1 Nov 2019) www.nytimes.com/2019/11/01/business/blizzcon-blizzard-protest.html accessed 15 December 2020.

Condis, Megan. *Gaming Masculinity: Trolls, Fake Geeks, and the Gendered Battle for Online Culture*. Minneapolis: University of Minnesota Press, 2018. Kindle edition.

Dechter, Gaci. *Wish You Weren't Here. The Baltimore Sun*. May 24, 2015.

Deshane, E. "Re-Imagining the Borderlands." *First Person Scholar*, 2017. http://www.firstpersonscholar.com/re-imagining/.

Diablo. Blizzard Entertainment, 1997.

Diablo II. Blizzard Entertainment, 2000.

Diablo III. Blizzard Entertainment, 2012.

Dune II. Westwood Studios, 1992.

Dürr, Eveline, and Rivke Jaffe. "Theorizing Slum Tourism: Performing, Negotiating and Transforming Inequality." *Revista Europea de Estudios Latinoamericanos y Del Caribe / European Review of Latin American and Caribbean Studies*, no. 93 (2012): 113–23. http://www.jstor.org/stable/23294474.

Dyer-Witheford, Nick and de Peuter, Greig. *Games of Empire: Global Capitalism and Video Games*. Minneapolis: University of Minnesota Press, 2009. Kindle edition.

The Elder Scrolls V: Skyrim. Bethesda Game Studios, 2011.

The Elder Scrolls Wiki. https://elderscrolls.fandom.com/wiki/The_Elder_Scrolls_Wiki.

The Elder Scrolls Skyrim: Special Edition Wiki.https://en.uesp.net/wiki/Skyrim:Special_Edition.

Eskelinen, Markku. "The Gaming Situation." *Game Studies: The International Journal of Computer Game Research* 1, No. 1 (July 2001). http://www.gamestudies.org/0101/eskelinen/.

EverQuest, Daybreak Game Company, 1999.

Fernández Ruiz, M., García-Reyes, D. "*Blacksad: Under the Skin.* Transmedia and Ludification as Cultural Experience." *evista de Comunicación*, 2021, vol. 20, No 2. 131–147.

Flanagan, Mary. *Critical Play: Radical Game Design.* Cambridge, Mass: The MIT Press, 2009.

Flanders, Stephanie. "Capital in the Twenty-First Century by Thomas Piketty – Review." *The Guardia*, 2014. https://www.theguardian.com/books/2014/jul/17/capital-twenty-first-century-thomas-piketty-review.

Frye, Northrop. *The Secular Scripture: A Study of Romance.* Cambridge: Harvard University Press, 1978.

Galloway, Alexander R. "Social Realism in Gaming." *Game Studies: The International Journal of Computer Game* 4, no. 1 (November 2004). http://www.gamestudies.org/0401/galloway/.

Game Studies: The International Journal of Computer Games Research. http://gamestudies.org.

Gee, J. P. *Good Video Games + Good Learning: Collected Essays on Video Games, Learning and Literacy.* New York: Peter Lang. 2007.

Genette, Gerald. *Narrative Discourse: An Essay in Method.* Translated by Jane E. Lewin. Ithaca: Cornell University Press, 1980.

Geraci, Robert M. *Virtually Sacred: Myth and Meaning in* World of Warcraft *and* Second Life. New York: Oxford University Press, 2014. Kindle edition.

Gordon, Robert J. *The Rise and Fall of American Growth.* Princeton: Princeton University Press, 2017. Kindle edition.

Grand Theft Auto: San Andreas. Rockstar, 2005.

Gray, Kishonna and Leonard, David J. *Woke Gaming: Digital Challenges to Oppression and Social Injustice.* Seattle: University of Washington Press, 2018. Kindle edition.

Green, Amy M. *Posttraumatic Stress Disorder, Trauma, and History in Metal Gear Solid Five.* Palgrave, 2017a. Kindle edition.

———. *Storytelling in Video Games: The Art of Digital Narrative.* McFarland, 2017b. Kindle edition.

"*Hamlet on the Holodeck: The Future of Narrative in Cyberspace.*" Kirkus, 1997. https://www.kirkusreviews.com/book-reviews/janet-h-murray/hamlet-on-the-holodeck/.

Harvey, David. *The Conditions of Postmodernity: An Enquiry into the Origins of Cultural Change.* Wiley-Blackwell, 1991.

Hearthstone. Blizzard Entertainment, 2014.

Hertz, J.C. *Joystick Nation: How Videogames Gobbled Our Money, Won Our Hearts and Rewired our Minds.* Little, Brown and Company 1997.

Herzog Zweil. Technosoft, 1990.

Hill, David W. Avatar Ethics: Beyond Images and Signs. Journal for Cultural Research Vol 17, No 1 (2013) 69–84.

Hawreliak, Jason. "Hybrid Publishing: The Case for the Middle State." *First Person Scholar*, 2013. http://www.firstpersonscholar.com/the-case-for-the-middle-state/.

Hayden, Craig. "The Procedural Rhetorics of Mass Effect: Video Games as Argumentation in International Relations." *International Studies Perspectives* (2017): 175–193.

Higgins, David M. "Dreams of Accumulation: The Economics of SF Video Games." *Science Fiction Studies* 43, no. 1 (2016): 51–66. https://doi.org/10.5621/sciefictstud.43.1.0051.

Jayemanne, Darshana. *Performativity in Art, Literature, and Videogames*. Palgrave Macmillan, 2017. Kindle edition.

Juul, Jesper. "Games Telling Stories?" *Game Studies: The International Journal of Computer Game Research* 1, No. 1 (July 2001). http://gamestudies.org/0101/juul-gts/.

———. *Half-Real: Video Games Between Real Worlds and Fictional Rules*. Cambridge, Mass: The MIT Press, 2005. Kindle edition.

Kennedy, Helen W. "Laura Croft: Feminist Icon or CyberBimbo: On the Limits of Textual Analysis" *Game Studies: The International Journal of Computer Game Research* 2, No. 2 (December 2002).

Keogh, Brendan. *A Play of Bodies: How We Perceive Videogames*. Cambridge, Mass: The MIT Press, 2018. Kindle edition.

Kocurek, Carly A. *Coin-Operated Americans: Rebooting Boyhood at the Video Game Arcade* Minneapolis: University of Minnesota Press, 2015. Kindle edition.

Krcmar, Marina and Drew P. Cingel. "Moral Foundations Theory and Moral Reasoning in Video Game Play: Using Real-Life Morality in a Game Context." *Journal of Broadcasting & Electronic Media* 60(1), 2016, pp. 87–103.

Krobová, T., Moravec, O., & Švelch, J. (2015). Dressing Commander Shepard in pink: Queer playing in a heteronormative game culture. *Cyberpsychology: Journal of Psychosocial Research on Cyberspace, 9*(3), Article 3. https://doi.org/10.5817/CP2015-3-3.

Krstić, Igor. "Remediating the 'Other Half': Planet Slum as Transmedia Project" In *Global Cinematic Cities: New Landscapes of Film and Media*. Edited by Johan Andersson and Lawrence Webb, 178–198. New York Chichester, West Sussex: Columbia University Press, 2016. https://doi.org/10.7312/ande17746-011.

Kucklich, Julian. "Perspectives on Computer Game Philology" Game Studies: The International Journal of Computer Game Research 3, No. 1 (May 2003). http://www.gamestudies.org/0301/kucklich/.

Leonard, A.A. "Video Games in Education: Why They Should Be Used and How They Are Being Used." *Theory into Practice* 47, no 3. (Summer 2008) 229–239 Taylor & Francis. (2008).

Leonard, D. J. "Not a Hater, Just Keepin' It Real: The Importance of Race- and Gender-Based Game Studies." *Games and Culture* 1 (2006): 83–88.

Lesage, Frédérik. Cultural Biographies and Excavations of Media: Context and Process Journal of Broadcasting & Electronic Media 57(1), 2013, 81–96.

Leyner, Mark. *Gone With the Mind.* Little, Brown, 2016. Kindle edition.

The Lost Vikings. Blizzard Entertainment, 1992.

MacCallum-Steward, Ester. "*Ready Player Two: Women Gamers and Designed Identity*, by Shira Chess." *Times Higher Education*, 2017. https://www.timeshighereducation.com/books/review-ready-player-two-shira-chess-university-of-minnesota-press.

Madden, Toby. "Synthetic Worlds: The Business and Culture of Online Games, Book Review." Federal Reserve Bank of Minneapolis, 2006. https://www.minneapolisfed.org/article/2006/synthetic-worlds-the-business-and-culture-of-online-games.

Maloney, Marcus and Steven, Robert. *Gender, Masculinity and Video Gaming: Analyzing Reddit's r/gaming Community.* Palgrave, 2019. Kindle edition.

Martoncik, Marcel and Loksa, Jan. "Do World of Warcraft (MMORPG) players experience less loneliness and social anxiety in online world (virtual environment) than in real world (offline)?" *Computers in Human Behavior* 56 (March 2015): 127–134.

McCaffery, Larry. *Avant-Pop: Fiction for a Daydream Nation.* Black Ice Books, 1992

———, eds. *After Yesterday's Crash: The Avant-Pop Anthology.* Penguin, 1995.

McDaniel, Rudy. *Literary and Linguistic Computing*, Volume 23, Issue 4, December 2008, Pages 502–504, https://doi.org/10.1093/llc/fqn029

Neuman, Michael Z. *Atari Age: The Emergence of Video Games in America.* Cambridge, Mass: MIT Press, 2017. Kindle edition.

Moberly, K. and Moberly, B. "There is no word for work in the dragon tongue." *The Year's Work in Medievalism, 28* (2013): 1–9.

Moria. Grabiner, 1988.

Mortensen, Torill. "Playing With Player's Potential: Methodologies for Muds" *Game Studies: The International Journal of Computer Game Research* 12, No. 1 (July 2002). http://www.gamestudies.org/0102/mortensen/.

Mukherjee, Souvik. *Video Games and Storytelling: Reading Games and Playing Books.* Palgrave Macmillan, 2015. Kindle edition.

Murray, Janet H. *Hamlet on the Holodeck: The Future of Narrative in Cyberspace.* Free Press, 1997. Kindle edition.

Neverwinter Nights, BioWare, 2002.

Nichols, Randy. *The Video Game Business.* British Film Institute, 2014.

NYMG: Feminist Game Studies. https://www.nymgamer.com/.

Orme, Stephanie. "Gaming at the edge: sexuality and gender at the margins of gamer culture." *Feminist Media Studies*, 16(2), (2016) pp. 374–375. Kindle edition.

Ouellette, Marc A. and Thomson, Jason C. *The Post 9/11 Video Game: A Critical Examination*. McFarland, 2017. Kindle edition.

Pearce, Alyssa Maria. "Exploring Performance of Gendered Identities through Language in *World of Warcraft*." *International Journal of Human–Computer Interaction*, 33:3, (2017) 180–189, https://doi.org/10.1080/10447318.2016.1230965.

Piero, Mike and Marc C. Ouellette, eds. *Being Dragonborn: Critical Essays on* The Elder Scrolls V: Skyrim. McFarland, 2021.

Piketty, Thomas. *Capital in the Twenty-First Century*. Boston: Harvard University Press, 2014. Kindle edition.

Punday, Daniel. Involvement, Interruption, and Inevitability: Melancholy as an Aesthetic Principle in Game Narratives Substance #105, Vol 33, no.3, 2004.

Queer Game Studies. Edited by Bonnie Ruberg and Adrienne Shaw. Minneapolis: University of Minnesota Press, 2017. Kindle edition.

Racing Destruction Set. EA Originals, 1985.

Radical Psycho Machine Racing. Blizzard Entertainment, 1991.

Reichlin, Bruno. (2001) Figures of Neorealism in Italian Architecture (Part 1). *Grey Room 05*, Fall 2001, 80.

Rock N Roll Racing. Blizzard Entertainment, 1993.

Rowlands, Timothy, et al. "Power, Violence and The Mask: Representations of Criminal Subjectivities in Grand Theft Auto Online." *Woke Gaming: Digital Challenges to Oppression and Social Injustice*. Eds. Kishonna Gray and David J Leonard. Seattle: University of Washington Press, 2018. 45–64.

Rubin, Joan Shelley. *The Making of Middlebrow Culture*. Chapel Hill: University of North Caroline Press, 1992. Kindle edition.

Ryan, Marie-Laurie. "Beyond Myth and Metaphor: The Case of Narrative in Digital Media." Game Studies: The International Journal of Computer Game Research 1, No. 1 (July 2001). http://www.gamestudies.org/0101/ryan/

Second Life. Linden Lab, 2003.

Shaw, Adrienne. *Gaming at the Edge: Sexuality and Gender at the Margins of Gamer Culture*. Minneapolis: University of Minnesota Press, 2015. Kindle edition.

Sicart, Miguel. Moral Dilemmas in Computer Games. *Design Issues:* Volume 29, Number 3 (2013).

Simon, Bart. "Difficult Writing." First Person Scholar (2016). http://www.firstpersonscholar.com/difficult-writing/

The Sims. Electronic Arts, 2000.

Skardzius, Karen, "Playing with Pride: Claiming Space Through Community Building in *World of Warcraft*." *Woke Gaming: Digital Challenges to Oppression and Social Injustice*. Eds. Kishonna Gray and David J Leonard. Seattle: University of Washington Press, 2018. 45–64. 175–192

Smith, Philip E. "The Mission of Rhetoric and the Rhetoric of Mission Statements." ADE Bulletin, no 121. (Winter 1998): 30–36.

Smith Stacy L. "Popular Video Games: Quantifying the Presentation of Violence and Its Context" Journal of Broadcasting & Electronic Media 46(1), 2003, 58–76.

Snodgrass, Jeffrey G. "Online virtual worlds as anthropological field sites: Ethnographic methods training via collaborative research of Internet gaming cultures." *Annals of Anthological Practice* 40, no. 2 (November 2016): 134–147.

StarCraft. Blizzard Entertainment, 1998.

StarCraft II. Blizzard Entertainment, 2010.

Stark, David K. "Grand Theft Architecture: Architectural Works in Video Games after E.S.S. Entertainment v. Rockstar Games," Berkeley Technology Law Journal 25, no. 1 (2010): 429–464.

Stigsdotter, Ingrid. "British Audiences and 1990s French New Realism." Je t'aime…moi non plus: Franco-British cinematic relations. Edited by Lucy Mazdon and Catherine Wheatley. Berghahn Books, 2010. 169–184.

Taylor, Laurie. "When Seams Fall Apart Video Game Space and The Player." Game Studies: The International Journal of Computer Game Research 3, No.2 (December 2003) http://www.gamestudies.org/0302/taylor/.

Thabet, Tamer. *Video Game Narrative and Criticism: Playing the Story*. Palgrave, 2015. Kindle edition.

"Thomas Piketty's *Capital* Summarized in Four Paragraphs." *The Economist*, 2014.https://www.economist.com/the-economist-explains/2014/05/04/thomas-pikettys-capital-summarised-in-four-paragraphs.

United Nations. "The Poverty of Poverty Measurement." https://www.un.org/esa/socdev/rwss/docs/2010/chapter3.pdf

Victor, Daviel 'Why Are People Protesting in Hong Kong' (New York Times, 19 Nov 2019) www.nytimes.com/2019/11/13/world/asia/hong-kong-protests.html accessed 15 December 2020.

Vossen, Emma "Academic Vigilantism." *First Person Scholar*, 2016a. http://www.firstpersonscholar.com/academic-vigilantism-and-middle-state-publishing/

———. "Publish or Perish: Or Publish with Purpose." *First Person Scholar* (2016b). http://www.firstpersonscholar.com/publish-or-perish/.

Wark, McKenzie. *Gamer Theory*. Boston: Harvard University Press, 2007. Kindle edition.

Welsh, Timothy J. *Mixed Realism: Videogames and the Violence of Fiction*. Minneapolis: University of Minnesota Press, 2016. Kindle edition.

World of Warcraft. Blizzard Entertainment. 2004.

Warcraft II: Tides of Darkness. Blizzard Entertainment, 1995.

Warcraft III. Blizzard Entertainment, 2002.

Warcraft: Orcs & Humans. Blizzard Entertainment, 1994.

Wilcox, Steve. "On the Publishing Methods of Our Time: Mobilizing Knowledge in Game Studies" *Scholarly and Research Communication 6*, issue 3, (2015).

Index[1]

[1] Note: Page numbers followed by 'n' refer to notes.

A. Crowley, *Representations of Poverty in Videogames*,
https://doi.org/10.1007/978-3-031-00144-4

FSC
www.fsc.org
MIX
Papier | Fördert gute Waldnutzung
FSC® C083411

Kolibri 360 GmbH
Ferdinand-Jühlke-Straße 7
99095 Erfurt, Deutschland
produktsicherheit@kolibri360.de